# Bic Runga's
*Drive*

T0314568

# 33 1/3 Global

**33 1/3 Global**, a series related to but independent from **33 1/3**, takes the format of the original series of short, music-based books and brings the focus to music throughout the world. With initial volumes focusing on Japanese and Brazilian music, the series will also include volumes on the popular music of Australia/Oceania, Europe, Africa, the Middle East, and more.

## 33 1/3 Japan

Series Editor: Noriko Manabe

Spanning a range of artists and genres—from the 1970s rock of Happy End to technopop band Yellow Magic Orchestra, the Shibuya-kei of Cornelius, classic anime series *Cowboy Bebop,* J-Pop/EDM hybrid Perfume, and vocaloid star Hatsune Miku—**33 1/3 Japan** is a series devoted to in-depth examination of Japanese popular music of the twentieth and twenty-first centuries.

Published Titles:

Supercell's *Supercell* by Keisuke Yamada

*AKB48* by Patrick W. Galbraith and Jason G. Karlin

Yoko Kanno's *Cowboy Bebop Soundtrack* by Rose Bridges

Perfume's *Game* by Patrick St. Michel

Cornelius's *Fantasma* by Martin Roberts

Joe Hisaishi's *My Neighbor Totoro: Soundtrack* by Kunio Hara

Shonen Knife's *Happy Hour* by Brooke McCorkle

Nenes' *Koza Dabasa* by Henry Johnson

Yuming's *The 14th Moon* by Lasse Lehtonen

Forthcoming Titles:

Yellow Magic Orchestra's *Yellow Magic Orchestra* by Toshiyuki Ohwada

Kohaku utagassen: The Red and White Song Contest by Shelley Brunt

## 33 1/3 Brazil

Series Editor: Jason Stanyek

Covering the genres of samba, tropicália, rock, hip hop, forró, bossa nova, heavy metal and funk, among others, **33 1/3 Brazil** is a series devoted to in-depth examination of the most important Brazilian albums of the twentieth and twenty-first centuries.

Published Titles:

Caetano Veloso's *A Foreign Sound* by Barbara Browning

Tim Maia's *Tim Maia Racional Vols. 1 & 2* by Allen Thayer

João Gilberto and Stan Getz's *Getz/Gilberto* by Brian McCann

Gilberto Gil's *Refazenda* by Marc A. Hertzman

Dona Ivone Lara's *Sorriso Negro* by Mila Burns

Milton Nascimento and Lô Borges's *The Corner Club* by Jonathon Grasse

Racionais MCs' *Sobrevivendo no Inferno* by Derek Pardue

Naná Vasconcelos's *Saudades* by Daniel B. Sharp

Chico Buarque's First *Chico Buarque* by Charles A. Perrone

Forthcoming titles:

Jorge Ben Jor's *África Brasil* by Frederick J. Moehn

## 33 1/3 Europe

Series Editor: Fabian Holt

Spanning a range of artists and genres, **33 1/3 Europe** offers engaging accounts of popular and culturally significant albums of Continental Europe and the North Atlantic from the twentieth and twenty-first centuries.

Published Titles:

Darkthrone's *A Blaze in the Northern Sky* by Ross Hagen

Ivo Papazov's *Balkanology* by Carol Silverman

Heiner Müller and Heiner Goebbels's *Wolokolamsker Chaussee* by Philip V. Bohlman

Modeselektor's *Happy Birthday!* by Sean Nye

Mercyful Fate's *Don't Break the Oath* by Henrik Marstal

Bea Playa's *I'll Be Your Plaything* by Anna Szemere and András Rónai

Various Artists' *DJs do Guetto* by Richard Elliott

Czesław Niemen's *Niemen Enigmatic* by Ewa Mazierska and Mariusz Gradowski

Massada's *Astaganaga* by Lutgard Mutsaers

Los Rodriguez's *Sin Documentos* by Fernán del Val and Héctor Fouce
Édith Piaf's *Récital 1961* by David Looseley
Nuovo Canzoniere Italiano's *Bella Ciao* by Jacopo Tomatis
Iannis Xenakis' *Persepolis* by Aram Yardumian

Forthcoming Titles:
Amália Rodrigues's *Amália at the Olympia* by Lila Ellen Gray
Ardit Gjebrea's *Projekt Jon* by Nicholas Tochka
Vopli Vidopliassova's *Tantsi* by Maria Sonevytsky

### 33 1/3 Oceania

Series Editors: Jon Stratton (senior editor) and Jon Dale (specializing in books on albums from Aotearoa/New Zealand)

Spanning a range of artists and genres from Australian Indigenous artists to Māori and Pasifika artists, from Aotearoa/New Zealand noise music to Australian rock, and including music from Papua and other Pacific islands, **33 1/3 Oceania** offers exciting accounts of albums that illustrate the wide range of music made in the Oceania region.

Published Titles:
John Farnham's *Whispering Jack* by Graeme Turner
The Church's *Starfish* by Chris Gibson
Regurgitator's *Unit* by Lachlan Goold and Lauren Istvandity
Kylie Minogue's *Kylie* by Adrian Renzo and Liz Giuffre
Alastair Riddell's *Space Waltz* by Ian Chapman
Hunters & Collectors's *Human Frailty* by Jon Stratton
The Front Lawn's *Songs from the Front Lawn* by Matthew Bannister
Bic Runga's *Drive* by Henry Johnson

Forthcoming Titles:
Ed Kuepper's *Honey Steel's Gold* by John Encarnacao
The Dead C's *Clyma est mort* by Darren Jorgensen
Chain's *Toward the Blues* by Peter Beilharz
Hilltop Hoods' *The Calling* by Dianne Rodger
Screamfeeder's *Kitten Licks* by Ben Green and Ian Rogers
Luke Rowell's *Buy Now* by Michael Brown

# Bic Runga's
# *Drive*

Henry Johnson

Series Editors: Jon Stratton, UniSA Creative,
University of South Australia, and Jon Dale,
University of Melbourne, Australia

BLOOMSBURY ACADEMIC
NEW YORK • LONDON • OXFORD • NEW DELHI • SYDNEY

BLOOMSBURY ACADEMIC
Bloomsbury Publishing Inc

1385 Broadway, New York, NY 10018, USA
50 Bedford Square, London, WC1B 3DP, UK
29 Earlsfort Terrace, Dublin 2, Ireland

BLOOMSBURY, BLOOMSBURY ACADEMIC and the Diana logo are
trademarks of Bloomsbury Publishing Plc

First published in the United States of America 2023

Cover design: Louise Dugdale
Cover image © …

A catalog record for this book is available from the Library of Congress.

ISBN: HB: 978-1-5013-9004-3
PB: 978-1-5013-9003-6
ePDF: 978-1-5013-9006-7
eBook: 978-1-5013-9005-0

Typeset by Deanta Global Publishing Services, Chennai, India
Printed and bound in Great Britain

Series: 33 ⅓ Oceania

To find out more about our authors and books visit www.bloomsbury.com
and sign up for our newsletters.

# Contents

Contents

# Figures

# 1 Introduction

## Introduction

'Into Overdrive: Bic Runga was the face and sound of 1997' (Alexander 1998). These complimentary words are from the caption to a photograph of multi-talented musician Bic Runga in 1997 in a weekend New Zealand newspaper, the *Sunday News*. The accolade summarizes the rapid impact that Runga had already made in the New Zealand music industry as a result of her highly acclaimed debut album, *Drive* (1997). The album was an instant national success, entering the New Zealand album charts at the No. 1 position and remaining in the Top 50 for an impressive sixty-four weeks (Scapolo 2007, n.p.).[1] It paved the way for her career as one of New Zealand's most celebrated pop music performers.

The caption that begins the chapter was a play on words of the title of her album, celebrating Runga's meteoric rise to fame in many facets of the music scene, which she certainly dominated for much of 1997. She was in fact a songwriter,

---

[1] Internationally, *Drive* peaked at No. 50 in the Australian charts in 1998. Some of Runga's other releases in the 1990s achieved moderate success overseas, including her 'Sway' single, which reached No. 10 in the Australian charts in 1998, and No. 83 in the UK Charts in 1998. See https://australian-charts.com /showitem.asp?interpret=Bic+Runga&titel=Drive&cat=a;    https://australian -charts.com/showitem.asp?interpret=Bic+Runga&titel=Sway&cat=s;    and https://www.officialcharts.com/search/singles/sway/ (accessed 4 July 2022).

multi-instrumentalist (e.g. voice, drums, piano, guitar) and music producer, with each talent contributing to the success of *Drive* and her releases that followed. It is with such recognition that this book offers insight into Runga's route to the New Zealand Music Hall of Fame (Te Whare Taonga Pūoro o Aotearoa),[2] an accolade presented to her in 2016, and one that recognized her high-profile career for nearly two decades after her debut album, multiple music industry awards, and many achievements in New Zealand and overseas.[3]

Acknowledging Runga's significance in the field of New Zealand popular music, this book discusses her debut, self-produced album, *Drive* (Appendix 1). The study navigates the performer's rise to national stardom, musical style, accolades and performance achievements in New Zealand and overseas.

# Bic Runga: A short biography

Born in Christchurch, Aotearoa New Zealand, in 1976, Bic Runga (Briolette Kah Bic Runga) grew up in the suburb of Hornby and attended Cashmere High School. Runga's early performance experiences were at home, with her musical mother and two older sisters, in high-school bands, and through the Christchurch School of Instrumental Music ('Drive Home' 2017).[4] These three spheres of musical influence

---

[2] See https://www.musichall.co.nz/portfolio/bic-runga/ (accessed 21 March 2022).
[3] See Bic Runga's website: http://bicrunga.com/ (accessed 1 March 2022).
[4] See https://www.csm.org.nz/ (accessed 11 April 2022).

nurtured an environment of music making through familial sway, peer association, and community music education.

Actively involved in a high-school culture of music making, Runga participated in the national high-school popular music competition, Rockquest, on several occasions (Chapter 2). Subsequent to her appearance in Rockquest in 1993 as part of the popular music duo, Love Soup, which won the Christchurch regional final and achieved third place in the nationals, Runga moved to Auckland (New Zealand's largest city) in 1994 and focused on her solo career. After actively developing her performance profile, Runga was signed to Sony Music New Zealand in 1995. The same year, Sony released her five-track EP, 'Drive', and in 1996 released her single 'Bursting Through' in the lead-up to the New Zealand release of her album, *Drive*, the following year.

Runga's rise to Kiwi stardom is acknowledged in her number of awards and nominations in the Aotearoa Music Awards (New Zealand Music Awards).[5] First appearing at the awards in 1996, when she was nominated for 'Most Promising Female' and 'Rising Star Award', she won the former category. Towards the end of the year, she was awarded the prestigious APRA Silver Scroll (Australasian Performing Right Association), an industry recognition of her songwriting for 'Drive'. A year later, Runga received three nominations in the Aotearoa Music Awards, winning the 'Female' award, and in 1998, reflecting the success of her album, *Drive*, she was nominated for and won

---

[5]In 1996 and 1997, the awards were known as the Clear Music and Entertainment Awards, and in 1999 as the New Zealand Music Awards. See https://aotearoamusicawards.nz/award-history/ (accessed 1 March 2022).

four awards: 'Album of the Year', 'Female', 'Single of the Year', and 'Songwriter'. Several other personnel on the album also received awards: Wayne Conway for the *Drive* album cover, and Simon Sheridan as the engineer. With this considerable foundation, and releasing further acclaimed albums (Appendix 2), Runga went on to win numerous other awards in the years that followed (the most of any individual New Zealand musician), which culminated in a Legacy Award in 2016 and her induction into the New Zealand Music Hall of Fame (Roach 2015).

After the release of *Drive*, the popularity of Runga's albums over the next decade is shown in Table 1.1, where the impact of her studio and live albums is clearly recognized. Her second studio album, *Beautiful Collision* (2002), released five years later, consolidated her acclaim by achieving a record 101 weeks in the charts and receiving recognition at the 2003 Aotearoa Music Awards ('Female', 'Highest Selling New Zealand Album', 'Producer', 'Solo Artist') (Aotearoa Music Awards 2020). But it

**Table 1.1** *Bic Runga in the Top 50 New Zealand Album Charts*

| Album | Year | Peak | Weeks in the Charts |
|---|---|---|---|
| *Drive* | 1997 | 1 | 64 |
| *Together in Concert: Live (Tim Finn, Bic Runga, Dave Dobbyn)* | 2000 | 2 | 26 |
| *Beautiful Collision* | 2002 | 1 | 101 |
| *Birds* | 2005 | 1 | 30 |

Source: Scapolo (2007, n.p.).

is with her debut album that Runga's career was propelled into the mainstream New Zealand music industry and she soon became a 'household name in New Zealand' (Moses 2017). Since its release, the album has achieved seven times platinum.[6] Some of its songs have been released as singles, featured in movies and become iconic sounds in the New Zealand music scene. As a debut album, such recognition is particularly relevant when considering Runga's key achievements en route to the New Zealand Music Hall of Fame (Table 1.2). From winning a regional high-school music competition to being honoured with the New Zealand Order of Merit, Bic Runga has attained an esteemed place within contemporary popular music. It is for such reasons that this book focuses on the album *Drive*.

In New Zealand, several single releases are connected with *Drive*, and in various ways. Two years before the album's release in New Zealand in July 1997, an EP version of the song 'Drive' was released, which is a slightly different version to the track of the same name on the album. Also on the EP is a version of Runga's song, 'Swim', which is noticeably different to the version of 'Swim' on the album (changing from a funky sound on the EP to a futuristic rock style on the album). Other New Zealand singles released from (or with versions on) *Drive* were 'Bursting Through' (September 1996),[7] 'Sway' (May 1997), 'Suddenly Strange' (September 1997) and 'Roll Into One'

---

[6]In New Zealand, platinum certification is awarded with sales of 15,000 units. See Recorded Music New Zealand: https://nztop40.co.nz/about (accessed 21 March 2022).
[7]Month and years indicate when the singles entered the New Zealand Top 50 charts.

**Table 1.2** *Key Achievements: From School to Stardom*

| Year | Achievement |
| --- | --- |
| 1993 | Winner of Canterbury regional final of Rockquest |
| 1993 | Third place in national final of Rockquest |
| 1994 | Moved to Auckland (worked in record shop) |
| 1995 | TV presenter on *Music Nation* |
| 1995 | Signed to Sony Music |
| 1995 | 'Drive' (Love Soup) EP released |
| 1996 | Most Promising Female Vocalist award for the song 'Bursting Through' |
| 1996 | APRA Silver Scroll award for the song 'Drive' |
| 1997 | Featured on the front cover of *New Zealand Musician* |
| 1997 | Featured on the front cover of *Rip It Up* |
| 1997 | Release of debut solo album, *Drive* |
| 1997 | Female Vocalist award (for 1996) |
| 1998 | Album of the Year award (for 1997) |
| 1999 | International Achievement award (for 1998) |
| 1999 | 'Sway' features in the movie, *American Pie* |
| 2000 | International Achievement award (for 1999) |
| 2006 | New Zealand Order of Merit |
| 2012 | 'Sway' features in the movie, *American Reunion* |
| 2016 | New Zealand Herald Legacy Award |
| 2016 | Inducted into the New Zealand Music Hall of Fame |
| 2017 | *Drive* re-released (20th-Anniversary Edition) |

(December 1997), the first two of which were re-recorded for the album.[8]

# Focus

One year before the release of Runga's 'Drive' EP of 1995, and as an accompanying volume to the then recently launched journal, *Perfect Beat* (from 1992), Hayward, Mitchell and Shuker published a collection of essays that aimed 'to document the nature of the music business in New Zealand, its associated media industries and the styles of music produced since the 1960s' (1994, i). While the collection didn't mention Bic Runga as she was just starting out in the music industry, it does help to show the mediatized framework interwoven with the New Zealand music scene at the time Runga gained mainstream attention. This includes a do-it-yourself outlook, supporting local music, and a desire to move beyond the marginal borders of the national music scene (Shuker 1994). Such parameters also reflected Runga's place and musical identity in a rapidly changing industry from a New Zealand perspective (Johnson 2010; Keam and Mitchell 2011). For example, in the mid-1990s, Runga was starting out as a performer, but had the help of success in a competition behind her, as well as her expeditious signing to a major multi-national label. The 1990s also saw increased top-down government funding and initiatives for the promotion of New Zealand popular music, of which Runga

---

[8]Other singles, sometimes with different combinations of additional tracks, were released internationally, including 'Sorry' and 'Hey'. There are also songs on some singles that didn't make the album.

had been a recipient, and she followed in the footsteps of many other New Zealand performers by advancing her career locally and overseas (Shuker 2001, 79).

In such a context, this book offers insight into the creative and industry processes that helped place Runga at the heart of New Zealand's popular music scene in the late 1990s. Focusing on the New Zealand release of *Drive*,[9] this book discusses the rise of Bic Runga as an icon of New Zealand popular music with the aim of outlining key themes around the making and promotion of her debut album. As a historical contribution to popular music studies, and informed by a plethora of published interviews and secondary sources, this book outlines Runga's early career with a focus on the years around the release of *Drive*, particularly from the mid- to late 1990s. While knowledge of her debut album has been discussed elsewhere, and most notably by Moses (2017), which includes a detailed commentary to celebrate the album's twentieth anniversary, I offer further insight based on a critical review of disparate sources (academic and general), as well as a discussion of key songs as case studies within each chapter. My study is particularly interested in discerning from different perspectives how *Drive* set the scene for Runga's numerous achievements in the music industry. As such, the book draws on musical biography as a method (Pekacz 2006), including personal communication with the performer and other personnel, and adopting a critical approach when discussing

[9]The album was released internationally between 1997 and 1998. A twentieth-anniversary edition was released in 2017.

the production, distribution, and consumption of Runga's early commercial songs.

Blending ideas from popular music studies with media analysis, the book is the first to offer a detailed study of Runga's creativity in the context of album production and the industry demands that go with this. In the discussion, the themes of identity and creative authenticity are foregrounded as prominent concepts when attempting to comprehend Runga's position as an artist, where each exists in a contested space between her creative expression on the one hand and her commercial brand on the other (Hall 1996; Moore 2002; Moorefield 2005; Zagorski-Thomas 2014). As such, and within the limited boundaries of this particular book, the discussion offers a glimpse into Runga's route to her place in the New Zealand Music Hall of Fame.

# Structure

This book identifies key themes that set the scene for Runga's rise to national stardom. The first of these, as outlined in this chapter, covers Runga's key achievements in the music industry, offering an overview of albums and accolades. Looking at Runga's break into commercial popular music, the subject of Chapter 2 is the high-school music competition, Rockquest, which provided the setting for Runga's entry into the professional music business. This chapter critiques the context of such competitions within the national pop music scene, along with other accolades bestowed upon the artist. Chapter 3 is a discussion of *Drive* and beyond, comprehending Runga's route to achieving national success. Runga brings a distinct identity to New Zealand music. Being of Māori and Malaysian Chinese descent, her ethnicity has been a subject in interviews and reviews. This theme is discussed in Chapter 4 in connection with New Zealand's multicultural setting in a bicultural political milieu, which is a distinct characteristic of Aotearoa New Zealand identity. The last main analytical chapter is a discussion of Runga's performance career, covering national and international spheres, and exploring the music industry processes that were a necessary part of her developing a career beyond New Zealand's marginal borders.

As a way of including knowledge about some of the album's songs, the book's main chapters include short case studies of the New Zealand singles released from (or leading to) the album (one each in Chapters 2 to 4, and two in Chapter 5). These five case studies – varying in length and content – provide a chronological and analytical study of key songs on this epoch-making album that launched Runga's musical career.[10] The case studies focus on the songs as found on the album, but discussion is included on some of the different versions of the songs as released on singles or elsewhere as a way of showing Runga's regular reimagining of her music.

## Summary

This chapter has introduced the significance of Bic Runga in the sphere of popular music in New Zealand in the 1990s,

---

[10]For a harmonic analysis of some of Runga's songs, see Braae (2012). For several notations of her songs, see *Nature's Best* (2002), *Nature's Best 2* (2004) and Runga (2006).

along with the relevance of discussing her debut album as the focus of this book. Within just a few years, and having only just left high school, Runga was propelled into New Zealand's popular music limelight and was a new star in 1997. Instrumental to her rise to fame were success in a high-school music contest, her signing to Sony and the immediate success of *Drive* among New Zealand fans.

The discussion in the following chapters consolidates the ideas presented here, particularly in connection with the themes of identity and creative authenticity, each of which is seen as a notion that helps in comprehending how Runga placed herself within commercial popular music. Starting in the lead-up to her success, Chapter 2 explores Runga's break into the professional music industry. The discussion offers insight into some of the many facets of the music business that helped her on her successful journey, taking Rockquest, her EP and her accolades as a starting point for discerning her route to becoming a leading light in New Zealand popular music.

# 2 Break

## Introduction

Bic Runga entered New Zealand's commercial popular music scene in the mid-1990s. This period in her career is characterized in terms of a balance between her musical creativity and music industry intervention (Long and Barber 2017). This polarity is typical of the pop music world, where bands negotiate a space between their musical ideas and the consumer industry that is integral to their commercial success (Shuker 2005, 180).

Between 1993 and 1999, four pivotal stages helped Runga's early success: (i) industry recognition in a national high-school music competition, (ii) the commercial release of an EP and its subsequent chart success, (iii) receiving national music awards and (iv) achieving a chart-topping debut album. Runga's break into the national music industry is discussed in both this chapter and the next over these four themes, which detail a short period that saw her move from high-school amateur musician to national icon in the commercial music sphere as a result of the blending of personal drive and music industry agency. Such a polarity often besets aspiring songwriters and raises questions concerning a performer's desire to maintain artistic ownership over their creative work while at the same time navigating the commercially driven world of contemporary popular music. In this context, the discussion explores the interconnection between Runga's authority over her creative work and the popular music industry that is driven by consumer commodification.

A case study of the song 'Drive' is included later in the chapter, which provides a succinct analysis focusing on the song's background, lyrics and music. The study helps show an example of Runga's early creativity (her first single was a prior production of the song), along with the commercially driven industry in which she started to work.

# Rockquest

Rockquest is a grassroots high-school popular music contest in New Zealand.[1] This national competition, which has regional heats, had its beginnings in 1988 when Christchurch radio station C93FM held a local event showcasing emerging pop music talent in the city (Arts Online 2021b; 'Smokefreerockquest 2013' n.d.). The competition was meant to be held again the following year, but the radio station pulled out. However, at the time, two school music teachers, Glenn Common and Pete Rainey, stepped in to organize the event because they already had school bands booked to perform.[2] Rockquest was subsequently established in 1989 and has continued annually to become a significant event in the lives of aspiring high-school musicians. As the organization notes,

---

[1] See https://smokefreerockquest.co.nz/ (accessed 3 May 2022).
[2] In recognition of Common's and Rainey's contribution to the New Zealand music industry through Rockquest, each were named Members of the New Zealand Order of Merit in 2013. They received further recognition of their work with Rockquest in 2021 with an Independent Spirit Award through Independent Music New Zealand.

it is 'New Zealand's biggest youth participation event, and the country's only nationwide, live, all original music competition' ('Smokefreerockquest 2013' n.d.).

Rockquest receives regional and national media prominence and is held in high esteem in the popular music sphere of youth culture and among high-school music teachers. As one eminent musician whose band won an award at the event in 2000 said: 'Rockquest is the pinnacle of music events for young [N]ew Zealanders. It also allows young songwriters to network and interact with, not only each other, but also accomplished artists to further develop their craft, and to gain a sense of pride and confidence in your own ability' (Feleti Strikson-Pua of Nesian Mystik, in Arts Online 2021a). The list of other successful New Zealand popular musicians and bands who have come through Rockquest is impressive, and includes The Datsuns, Anika Moa, King Kapisi, Fur Patrol, Steriogram, Brooke Fraser and Evermore. For these artists and others, Rockquest has offered a competitive and performative space for aspiring musicians to gain experience and to use as a springboard for potential commercial success.

Evolving quickly, in 1990, Rockquest Promotions was formed and, with a major international sponsor, the Coca-Cola Rockquest was born (named sponsorship has varied over the years). The event now comprised five regional competitions (Auckland, Wellington, Christchurch, Dunedin and Rotorua), which reflected four main urban areas, along with Rotorua with its substantial Māori population,[3] plus a national final. A

---

[3] See Statistics New Zealand: https://www.stats.govt.nz/tools/2018-census -place-summaries/rotorua-district (accessed 25 May 2022).

year later, the event became the Smokefree Rockquest, with a one-hour national show on TV2, reinforcing its increasing popularity across the nation. Further regional competitions were added with nine taking part in 1994 and twelve by 1996. Further sponsorship and growing popularity saw fifteen regionals by 1998, which included almost 500 entries, and eighteen regionals by 1999. Continued regional involvement saw twenty regionals in 2001, comprising 600 entries and an award-winning series of three TV shows (this grew to five the following year).[4]

The growth of Rockquest was partly a result of its own model that filled a gap for emerging young performers, and later offered a youth alternative in the broader commercial sphere to the local competition *Popstars* and other emerging international shows and local franchises that followed a similar format and had gained widespread media and consumer interest (e.g. *New Zealand Idol*, 2004; *New Zealand's Got Talent*, 2008; *X-Factor* [New Zealand], 2013).

Runga's early experiences of performing publicly were in Rockquest as a Cashmere High School student. She was an entrant in the second year of the competition, and four years later was a national finalist. As she comments: 'I first entered . . . when I was a third former in 1989 [Year 9/age 12–14]. Every year it became more and more serious, even for the kids just looking forward to seeing the show' (Runga 1998).[5] Her

[4] A cultural split in Rockquest occurred in 2000 with a Smokefree Pacifica Beats event added.
[5] Bic's older sister, Pearl, also entered the competition in 1989, as a member of the Hornby High School band, Outer Control ('All Keyed up for Rock Quest' 1989).

comments help show the importance of the contest among youth culture of the time, and especially for her.

In 1992, the Cashmere High School band, Judas Iscario, entered the Christchurch regional Rockquest final. An originals band, one of its five members was Bic Runga, their drummer and lead vocalist (Walker 1992). Other members of this youthful and ambitious band were Robin Wells (saxophone), Kelly Horgan (guitar), Dave Clark (guitar, vocals), and Jonny Langley (bass). This stage of Runga's musical career helped showcase her skills on the drums and voice, as well as her gendered position as the only female member of the band. Her place as the band's drummer helps to show not only her musical skills on this instrument, but also her determination as a female musician performing in a musical style that has typically been dominated by men (Hebert, Abramo and Smith 2017, 464). This positionality helped drive her musical ambitions to carve out a discrete place in New Zealand popular music, as well as helping to pave the way for a new wave of female New Zealand musicians inspired by her achievements.[6]

Bic Runga's final entry in Rockquest was in 1993, in her seventh form (Year 13/age 16–18), when she entered the regional competition in Christchurch as part of a girl-boy duo called Love Soup (Runga 1998; Sweet As Media Limited 2008a; b).[7] The other half of the duo was guitarist Kelly Horgan,[8] who had earlier played with Runga in their high-school band, Judas

---

[6] Rockquest has been a major influence in supporting original songs by young women, particularly with its Smokefree Women's Musicianship Award from 1993 ('Smokefreerockquest 2013' n.d.).

[7] Also written Lovesoup, as on the disk of her EP (Runga 1995).

[8] Horgan later played with The Heavy Jones Trio.

Iscario, as noted above (Mills and Howells 2020). Winning the Christchurch regional final, Runga's skills were acknowledged by a judge at the competition, Trevor Reekie of Pagan Records, who recognized Runga as 'remarkable' and a 'fearless performer' (Reekie, in Moses 2017).[9] As Love Soup, Runga and Horgan then traveled to Wellington for the national final, where they came third ('Infocus' 1993; New Zealand On Screen 2021).

Related talent shows have received much attention in popular music scholarship, especially in connection with television shows that include voting input from viewers (unlike Rockquest). For example, in Zwaan and de Bruin's (2012) collection of essays that critique the *Idols* TV series, various characteristics of authenticity are discussed in connection with the media authority that underpins the show and its attempt to portray its idols as creative acts. With Runga's homegrown exploits in a local music competition, however, the event was primarily concerned with showcasing emerging talent, rather than manipulating that talent for the TV screen. In other words, authenticity was inherent in her performances in terms of the lack of industry intervention in branding her sound and image. However, Rockquest had an immense influence on Runga, and, as a teenager, she was able to gain experience performing live in bands, entering contests and in crafting a performance persona. As she notes:

Rockquest has had an amazing effect on NZ music. Learning at high school level the art and craft of the rock band in an

---

[9] Reekie was guitarist in Car Crash Set in the 1980s and founder of the record labels Pagan and Antenna ('Trevor Reekie' 2021).

empirical competitive way was a big part of my school year. I think I entered it every time I was able to. It got me accustomed to being on stage and what makes an original song and a performance work. (Bic Runga 2021, pers. comm.)

After Reekie had seen Runga's performance in Christchurch, he invited her and Horgan to Wellington to make some recordings with himself and Nigel Stone. Reekie comments that 'anyone could see that she was incredibly talented' and he was 'just the first to recognize it' (Trevor Reekie 2022, pers. comm.). Even at that time in her career, Reekie realized that she 'was going to go somewhere . . . she had the motivation and her own belief . . . she had the strength of character . . . she had proven that by doing an acoustic set . . . she had the songs' (Trevor Reekie 2022, pers. comm.).

In Wellington, Stone was the sound engineer and several musicians collaborated on the recordings.[10] The session was extended to include a video of one of the songs, 'You' (3'32") (the second track on her EP), which only showed Runga on screen and therefore elevated her position in the duo to that of the front person (Runga 1994). However, rather than immediately launching her or Love Soup's professional musical career, the video was screened on TV just once.

As part of her break into the music industry, the recordings with Pagan were made with funding support from the Queen Elizabeth II Arts Council of New Zealand, and the video of 'You' was made with funding from New Zealand On Air. Runga and

---

[10]Bob Smith (keyboards), Trevor Reekie (keyboards, twelve-string guitar, acoustic guitar, e-bow), Greg Johnson (trumpet) and Richard Caigou (percussion).

Horgan actually wrote 'You' during their visit to Wellington. As Runga notes: 'we wrote ["You"] . . . when we were staying in the backpackers near the place we were going to record it. It's not a very typical song of the sort of thing we've been doing' (Runga, in Various Artists 1995b). The recording session created a juncture where her solo career outside of Love Soup was soon to take off, along with a rebranding of her musical image ('You' had already been featured on a promotional CD – Various Artists 1995a). It was at this point that Runga realized her potential to pursue a professional career in music (Runga, in Moses 2017): 'This was the old Bic and it wasn't what she or Sony wanted to present as her New Zealand debut [two years later]' (Gallagher 2013).

Following her Rockquest success, Runga moved to Auckland in 1994. As the largest city in New Zealand, and in 1994 with a population of 973,000,[11] her move from Christchurch – population of 322,000 in 1994 – was one that would put her in reach of a larger part of the local music industry. New Zealand's regional centres are hives of distinct local music activity, but they are by far overshadowed by the sheer population of Auckland, along with the city being the home to many organizations, companies and personnel in the music industry. Ultimately, this move helped Runga secure a major recording contract the following year, and reflects the necessity for many regional performers to move geographically to larger urban areas to seek success within the industry (Negus 2017, 158). As Runga confirms: 'There was no possibility of getting signed

---

[11] See https://www.macrotrends.net/cities/21957/auckland/population, https://www.macrotrends.net/cities/21958/christchurch/population (accessed 21 April 2022).

by a major record label in Christchurch, so the remoteness of the place not only inspired you to do something creative but also made you aspire to what was happening in a bigger city, which in my case was Auckland' (Runga, in Clayton-Lea 2004).

Over the next year, Runga worked at The CD Store,[12] and started work as a TV presenter on the show, *Music Nation* (New Zealand On Screen 2022). Maintaining a performing career in her spare time, she was signed to Sony Music in New Zealand in September 1995 (Dix 2005, 280). On her achievements at this time, Runga reflects on her youthfulness when signing with a major multinational record label as she was 'only two years out of high school' (Runga 1998).

Contact with Sony was made when Runga sent in a demo tape. As Paul Ellis, who was running A&R for Sony Music at the time, notes: 'I think there were four songs on the cassette and the last song was "Drive". I remember staring at the carpet, thinking "this is a life-changing song"' (Ellis, in Moses 2017). As part of the signing, Sony bought the Pagan recordings from Reekie and released them on Runga's EP of 1995 (Ellis, in Moses 2017). Typical of success in the music industry, it was at this stage in Runga's early career that her hard work and endurance paid off with a recording contract (Negus 2017, 160), yet at a juncture between amateur and professional musician, and embarking on a career driven by music industry agency. However, Runga strove to maintain a sense of authenticity in her music by including production in her list of many attributes, and it is with this additional level of creativity that

---

[12]On this store and other music stores in Auckland, see Grigg (2022).

she was able to ride a balance between artistic guardianship and industry intervention.

## 'Drive' EP

Pagan Records had a letter of intent with Runga (Moses 2017), but she was soon signed to Sony (Polson 1997, 5). With her demo recording of her song 'Drive' as the main track (Runga 1999b),[13] Epic Records (owned by Sony) released Runga's debut commercial recording in 1995, which was a five-track EP.[14]

Apart from the song 'Drive', the other songs on the EP were recorded with Pagan in Wellington at the Games Room venue in 1994.[15] The EP was made with the assistance of funding from the Queen Elizabeth II Arts Council (now Creative New Zealand), and her video of 'You' (1994) from the EP with help from New Zealand On Air (Runga 1994; 1995). As part of an initiative to help support local musicians where they might need funding, these New Zealand organizations have helped emerging artists in the field of popular music. In a study of such funding providers, Shuker notes that while initial support for performers was based on governmental initiatives, it was soon

---

[13] This version of the song was produced by Wayne Bell, who was later to play drums on Runga's album, *Drive*, and engineered by Chris van de Geer, who later played guitar in stellar* with Runga's sister, Boh. For the video version of the song with the EP soundtrack, see Runga (2011b).

[14] Epic was founded in 1953 in the United States, and while it started as a jazz and classical music label, it diversified over the years to include such artists as Michael Jackson, Ozzy Osbourne and Meghan Trainor.

[15] The Games Room is a bar and part of the event centre at Foxglove Bar & Kitchen.

driven 'by a more pragmatic concern for the economic value of the industry, especially in relation to its export potential' (2008, 271).

The front cover of the EP brands Runga simply as 'bic', with the CD's title given as 'drive' (all in lowercase). The physical disk itself gives the performer's full name, 'BIC RUNGA', with a title, 'LOVESOUP EP', written beneath (all in capital letters). This secondary title offers recognition of the duo that appeared in Rockquest. That is, apart from the song 'Drive', which has only Runga on guitar and vocals, Kelly Horgan features on guitar on the other four tracks.

On the EP's front cover, Runga sports bright-red lipstick, earrings and a collar neck cord. She is featured looking down and wearing leather trousers and a white T-shirt that blends with the CD's white background. The inside cover shows a similar photo, but this time she is wearing a dark long-sleeve top. While offering an image that captures Runga's femininity, in both photos the performer is looking down, not showing her eyes, which is a pose that seems to disconnect Runga from her audience and signifies a sense of mystery. With the image, Runga is disengaged, expressing thoughtfulness, independence and social distance. This is more a visualization of Runga the solo artist, part of a brand that was moving ahead in the music industry and leaving Love Soup behind.

Bannister discusses similar imagery in one of Runga's videos of 'Sway', where 'the camera looks at Bic, but she does not look back, rather her gaze is directed elsewhere' (2010, 87). Such a pose is found with Runga elsewhere in other photoshoots and interviews around this time. As one newspaper review notes: 'SELF-CONSCIOUSLY distant from cameras and photographers, Bic Runga is more absorbed with her music than herself. Awkwardly she reclines, looking away from the camera' ('Bic Expectations' 1997). It is with such a stance that Runga at this time is understood more through her music than her appearance. However, as discussed in Chapter 4, Runga's cultural identity has often been played out in the media, which, in the case of the EP's and album's imagery, is a further factor in signifying who she is.

Popular music inherently connects with many other cultural spheres, and album iconography offers multiple semiotic expressions of what performers and their music stand for. After all, 'artists need to tell us about themselves' (Machin 2010, 32). In the case of Runga's EP, the visual product is the performer, her debut release via a major record label and with an imagery that introduces Runga but keeps her veiled and asking the viewer to look deeper into the performer and her music.

The EP's tracks include two that were later featured on Runga's album of the same name, although re-recorded for the album: 'Drive' and 'Swim', the EP's opening and closing tracks respectively. Only one of the tracks, 'You', was co-written by Runga and Horgan, which, as noted previously, was also made into a video (Runga 1994). With the EP, and especially when considering its branding, by the time of its release, the Love Soup duo in the form that performed at Rockquest was now replaced by Bic Runga as a solo artist, albeit in a context with the EP being released as a musical remnant of the duo's high-school days.

# Music awards

Already enjoying the success of being the recipient of the 1996 Clear Music and Entertainment Awards' 'Most Promising Female Vocalist',[16] and nominated for its 'Rising Star Award', Runga's song 'Drive' was widely acclaimed and for it she was presented the prestigious 1996 APRA Silver Scroll 'Songwriting Award'. With such awards, the idea of gender is foregrounded (i.e. 'female'), as is 'songwriting'. While the latter is gender neutral, it had been awarded to a male songwriter on most other occasions (APRA AMCOS 2022).

The significant APRA award dates from 1965 and over the three decades prior to Runga receiving it, just three other women had won it (with Shona Laing winning it twice: 1988 and 1992). With five times the number of men winning it over these years, when the award goes to a female artist its significance is emphasized as a result of the historical gender imbalance of female awardees. This unevenness continued for a further ten years after Runga's award where New Zealand male songwriters had dominance. However, over the years after 2007 there was a more or less even gender division, also with some awards made to songwriting partnerships comprising male and female members.

Unmasking such gender disparity helps show a slow change in the recognition of New Zealand's female songwriters, where a once male-dominated industry now sees an increase in successful female artists. While such female performers as Shona Laing and Bic Runga have been firmly

---

[16] Now the Aotearoa Music Awards.

embedded in the national music industry from the 1980s and 1990s respectively, a new era of successful female performers such as Brooke Fraser, Lorde and Benee has emerged over the past few decades. While Runga's Silver Scroll award did not immediately change the gender imbalance of later awards, her achievement at the time did help pave the way for a new generation of female performers who have followed in her footsteps in being recognized as outstanding icons in the New Zealand music industry. As Trevor Reekie confirms, 'the effect that Bic has had on the current [as of 2017] glut of great female singer-songwriters is quite amazing' (Reekie, in Moses 2017).

In the years soon after releasing her EP, Runga was the recipient of a number of other music industry awards. In the 1997 New Zealand Music Awards, she won Female Vocalist and was nominated for Single of the Year and Best Songwriter for her follow-up single, 'Bursting Through', which was released towards the end of 1996. A year later, among an array of accolades, her album *Drive* was Album of the Year, and her single 'Sway' was Single of the Year. At the same awards she was the recipient of (best) Female and Songwriter with 'Sway'. The awards extended to the album's iconography and record production, with best Album Cover being awarded to Wayne Conway for *Drive*, and Best Engineer to Simon Sheridan for 'Sway'. The official video released for Runga's single, 'Suddenly Strange' of 1997, received a nomination for its director, Wayne Conway, for best Music Video. By 1999, Runga had further expanded her reach to an international market and was the recipient of the International Achievement award, which was the same year her older sister, Boh, won Most Promising Female.

These awards help show the New Zealand music industry's recognition of Runga's creative talent, and marked her entry into the upper echelon of New Zealand popular music. Over just a few years, Runga had moved from high-school Rockquest finalist to a Sony recording artist, from Christchurch to Auckland and then from Aotearoa to the international stage.

# Case study: 'Drive'

As released on her EP, Runga's song 'Drive' was a low-budget demo version she sent to Sony in her quest for a record label signing. As Runga notes: 'Back then, I gave Sony a demo tape that I'd recorded for about GBP20 [NZD40], basically just of me and an acoustic guitar, singing "Drive", and they decided to release it as it was, no re-recording. It made the top ten' (Runga, in Allen 1998). The single peaked at No. 10 and stayed in the New Zealand Top 50 charts for twelve weeks (Scapolo 2007, n.p.).

'Drive' was re-recorded for the album, although with only very slight differences; the two versions sound very similar. Both the EP and album versions feature Runga as singer-guitarist. The main differences are that the EP version is 3'01" and the album version is 2'48". The vocals are almost identical, but the guitar part has some minor variance with the album version omitting a note at the end of the finger-picking guitar pattern. In terms of Runga's overarching creativity, while the EP version was produced by Wayne Bell, who plays drums on eight tracks on *Drive*, the album version of the song was produced by Runga herself (she also mixed the song), thereby contributing a further element of her artistry and broader vision for how the song should sound.[17]

'Drive' was a pivotal song for Runga. The opening track of her EP of the same name, and also the opening track of her debut album with the same name, the instrumentation comprises Runga on voice and acoustic guitar. As the first song heard on the album, and with a dark, solemn feel, the track is different to the band line-up of all the other songs on the album, and for many artists might not have been the favoured opening track. However, 'Drive' provides a window into Runga's creative talent, through which the listener is then taken on a musical journey through the album's other sounds.

With the word 'drive' given prominence in these early releases, one might expect a deep engagement with cars or another meaning of the word (ambition, journey etc.). As she noted in an early promotional media release: 'I wrote a lot of songs in the car. . . . Drive is basically about driving. . . . It's one of my favourite things' (Runga, in NZ On Air 1996). The idea of cars does feature on the album, or in related imagery, in several ways (Figure 2.1). Visually, the album's liner notes have several photographs of road markings (turn right and lane dividers) and one with Runga looking out of a car's rear window. The album's back cover also shows white road markings, thereby emphasizing the idea of 'drive' as in driving a car. The songs on the album have several references to such visual representation. For example, the song 'Drive', while

---

[17] A band version of the song was recorded, which was produced by Wayne Bell, although not released (Bell, in Kennedy and McCrum 2020). The EP version of the song was also released on Various Artists (2002).

**Figure 2.1** *Singer Bic Runga. Shows her driving a car. Location unidentified. Photograph taken circa 23 December 1997 by* Evening Post *(Wellington) staff photographer Melanie Burford. Courtesy of Stuff and the Alexander Turnbull Library, Wellington, New Zealand.*

inherently signifying an image of a car, includes one significant line that reinforces the vehicle representation: 'Ride in your car now but please don't drop me home'; and the song 'Hey' has one line that adds to the imagery as an onlooker: 'Hanging out the window watching the cars passing by'.

Overall, such car imagery is evident more through street photography than in song lyrics, and the idea behind the song seems more abstract than representational. Indeed, Runga describes how and where she wrote 'Drive' as follows:

> It was written a few minutes before my first solo gig in Auckland – I didn't have enough songs to make up a 40 minute set. That's a good indication of the way I like to work, I work well under pressure and I think that the best songs write themselves. They don't feel labored over. The demo version was released as a single, and for the album we tried to record it lots of different ways but they didn't work. It has to be simple. (Runga 1999a)

'Drive' went on to be one of her most popular songs, showcasing the emerging artist's early talent as a singer-songwriter, multi-instrumentalist and producer. The two versions that appeared early in Runga's career reflect her re-working of songs in that other versions of 'Drive' are also in existence (Chapter 3).

As a love song, 'Drive' portrays a couple's ride in a car and includes expressions of longing and desire. While a car theme is reinforced with the inclusion of traffic markings in the album's liner notes, the lyrics are open to interpretation with layers of meaning, such as in the lines: 'When I ride with you' and 'Take me through make me feel alive'. A poetic part of the lyrics is found with the line 'Let rain fall from concrete coloured skies'. The place of this line in the song juxtaposes with the driving theme, and it actually replaced an earlier lyric, 'Rain falls like custard from the sky' (Songfacts 2021), which shows insight into Runga's imaginative poetics during the songwriting process.

Written in a 4/4 time signature with gentle finger-picking guitar accompaniment, Runga's voice articulates the lyrics and melody in a highly expressive way. The song's architecture is typical of popular music form and, unlike some songs with two opening verses, solos or modulations, Runga opted for a straightforward form as follows:

Verse | Chorus | Verse | Chorus | Chorus (part)

While such a form might reflect the relatively succinct amount of time she had to write the song, there are inherent songwriting skills, which, along with the introspective lyrics, help to show Runga's talent and her belief that 'the best songs write themselves' (Runga 1999a).

The verses are written each with sixteen bars. With the chorus, however, Runga has skillfully shortened the overall number of bars to fourteen. The chorus begins with a four-bar phrase, but where one might expect to hear further repetition across subsequent bars, as with the verse, the chorus then breaks down into two-bar phrases. While the verse consists of a repeated melody, the chorus introduces the catchphrase 'drive' and its rhyming 'alive', both of which dominate the melodic vocal line. With the ending of the song, Runga cuts the chorus short and finishes with a six-bar rendition that closes with a slightly altered cadential formula with the melodic line falling at the end of the song.

Creating a foundation below a minor melody, the harmony moves in a way that offers a sense of home key ambiguity. While each line of the verse begins with Dm7, the lines end on C. The BbMaj7 to C progression offers a sense of closing, as with b7 pop music harmony, but the cadential closure actually occurs from the last chord in the verse (C) to the first of the next line (Dm7), which again offers a b7 cadential formula.

Played on an acoustic guitar with a capo on the fifth fret, the song's harmonic language includes chord extensions (minor and major sevenths) that add a slight jazz flavour. There are just three chords to the entire song, but Runga offers different permutations on guitar that help propel the song through each verse and chorus. With the chorus, the harmony begins with a permutation of the same chords found in the verse, with three of them played in reverse to the verse: BbMaj7, C and Dm7 (two bars). The first two bars are repeated in the next line, but this is where Runga skillfully alters the chorus by omitting two bars that might normally be found. Instead, the chorus then moves to two lines using the same chords as the verse, which creates familiarity in the harmonic structure but with difference on the surface-level melodic line.

## Summary

This chapter has explored the early stage of Bic Runga's engagement with the New Zealand music industry. It has covered key points relating to her musical endeavours from amateur high-school musician to a professional and highly acclaimed singer-songwriter recording artist.

As a high-school student, Runga entered the nation's Rockquest competition and, while not winning the national final, was spotted as a potential recording artist and was soon working with an independent label. This was her first stage of moving from amateur to professional musician, although in the few years that followed the competition she maintained career interests elsewhere while recording first her EP and then her album. Runga's songwriting creativity is expressed clearly in her early songs. Her acoustically driven lounge style with folk, pop and jazz influences characterized her early success. This was soon recognized with national music industry awards, which were followed by a highly successful first album. These early years showed the transformation from amateur to professional artist, and help illustrate some of the polarities in the industry that performers negotiate in connection with a desire to make a career yet at the same time wanting to maintain the creative authenticity of their commercial product.

The case study of the song 'Drive' offered an analysis of its inspiration, lyrics and musical language, each of which helped illustrate Runga's early style and influences. Carefully crafted lyrics with multiple layers of meaning combine to help consolidate a musical style that became a hallmark of Runga's early career. The discussion now moves to look more closely at her album *Drive*, among other releases, and some of the details that made Runga's music what it was at this stage in her career.

# **3**  *Drive* and Beyond

## Introduction

A study of *Drive* provides insight into Bic Runga's songwriting, performance and production, but also offers knowledge about the music industry at the time of the album's release in 1997. Focusing on *Drive* as a pivotal and significant album in the making of Bic Runga the recording artist, this chapter documents and discusses Runga's musical output and style. It discerns key processes that Runga went through in making the album, along with distinct attributes that she provided, including her creative skills in songwriting, playing a number of instruments and production ability in having a vision for the album's entirety. The chapter closes with a short case study of the song 'Bursting Through'.

## Musical output

While *Drive* characterized Runga's style of the time, she also released other songs in this period that didn't feature on the album (e.g. released as additional tracks on singles). As discussed in Chapter 2, there was an EP of the same name, released in 1995 and providing a taste of what the album might offer. In addition, some of the album's songs have been re-released on other albums, most significantly on the twentieth-anniversary edition of *Drive* (2017c), which included four additional tracks: 'Dust' (from the 'Hey' single of 1998, which was an international release), 'All Fall Down' (from the 'Suddenly Strange' single of 1997), 'Close the Door, Put Out the Light' (also from the 'Hey' single) and 'Sway' (single mix).[1] In addition, in 1999, she released a single, 'Good Morning Baby', in collaboration with US country-rock musician Dan Wilson, which was featured in the 1999 film *American Pie*, along with her song 'Sway'.

Album titles often take the name of a key song that features as a single. With *Drive*, while the track 'Drive' was released as an EP, and the album opens with a re-recorded version of the song, as Runga comments, the album was essentially about a relationship break-up:

> There wasn't a theme at the time but looking back and thinking about the album's title Drive, I was very driven! A lot of the songs are break up songs, but they have an empowered theme in the break up story. This was congruous with wanting to self pen and self produce everything. (Bic Runga 2021, pers. comm.)

Runga's comments about wanting to write and produce everything play out in her creative authenticity, moving from songwriter to performer, and then to producer, which is a theme explored in more detail later in this chapter and in Chapter 4.

Runga's induction into the New Zealand Music Hall of Fame should be understood in connection with her wider

---

[1] There is also a 'Limited Edition' of *Drive*, featuring some tracks from her EP and other recordings (Runga 1999).

contribution to the New Zealand music industry.[2] Her musical output is impressive, and while studio albums are released infrequently, she has attained peer recognition as an icon of New Zealand popular music. Since *Drive*, four studio albums have followed (Appendix 2). There was a five-year gap between *Drive* and her follow-up album, *Beautiful Collision* (2002), which consolidated Runga's initial success, with the album also receiving critical acclaim, chart success and national awards.[3] Similar reception occurred with her third studio album, *Birds* (2005). It was a further six years, however, before she released *Belle* (2011a), which saw Runga offer a number of co-written songs, and a further five years before *Close Your Eyes* (2016), which comprised ten covers and just two of her own songs.

While exploring new creative avenues, the latter two albums didn't receive the acclaim of Runga's earlier releases. Clarifying the production of an album of mostly covers, Runga offered the following statement about *Close Your Eyes*: 'the songs that all made it on the record specifically say something about where I'm at in my life, better than if I'd written it myself. It was a challenging process' (Runga, in 'Listen' 2016). The album is also significant in that it was released one day after her induction into the New Zealand Music Hall of Fame. While maintaining her creative output at the time of this award, the release also offered an introspective view of how Runga sees her life as reflected through the songs of others.

---

[2] On popular music halls of fame, see Nowak and Baker (2018).
[3] A collaborative live album with Tim Finn and Dave Dobbyn was released in 2000 (*Together in Concert: Live*).

# Style and production

What is Runga's musical style? Does she have a particular musical expression? Can she be pigeonholed alongside other musicians? This part of the chapter offers an exploration of Runga's musical style and production work, a combination that quickly established the artist as an icon of New Zealand popular music.

**Style.** Concerning the authenticity of Runga's performance style early in her career, Trevor Reekie (Pagan Records) comments that her type of performance 'was totally genuine . . . coming from deep inside . . . you believe in it right away . . . that's rare' (Trevor Reekie 2022, pers. comm.). Such intimacy in performance was further noted during an early gig with Runga singing her song 'Drive' in a small-scale Auckland venue, when her soon-to-be-drummer Wayne Bell commented: 'It felt like she was singing to me . . . and it's not just me, it's everybody in this room . . . that is so powerful' (Bell, in Kennedy and McCrum 2020). Sweetman comments that the song 'speaks to New Zealanders and it speaks of a New Zealand experience, the boredom of being in a small town. Just being in the car, driving, makes the song's narrator feel alive' (2012, 117). It was with such talent that Runga's career was set to take off, which included an extraordinary presence across all spheres of the creative process.

In terms of her musical style, Runga's music falls into several categories. As commented on by New Zealand popular music scholar and musician Matthew Bannister:

Runga has stuck to classic 'pop' formats that are acceptable to a mainstream middle-class New Zealand audience. But within these parameters she has also been quite exploratory, ranging from guitar-based folky pop, the musical style that connotes locality most clearly to a Pākehā [European] audience, to classic '60s-style middle-of-the-road pop balladry à la Dusty Springfield or Dionne Warwick, and to bohemian songwriter/auteurs (e.g. Dylan and Cohen). (Bannister 2010, 89)

Even though some of her early songs included experimentation with contemporary mixes (discussed later), Bannister's description offers several categories and points to a moderate musical style. But even within this balladry there were explorations of different sounds, such as the country feel to 'Roll Into One' and the rock chorus of 'Hey'. With *Drive*, Runga was developing her sound while at the same time attempting to appeal to slightly different musical tastes. While especially characterized by her vocal style, which has been described as 'restrained, pure, clear, beautiful, and not using a lot of vibrato or melisma' (Bannister 2010, 89), even with this instrument, Runga is found singing in diverse ways on *Drive*, ranging from her belting voice in 'Hey' to her subdued, melancholic and sweet vocal style in 'Bursting Through'.

Runga's voice is part of her musical brand, as is performing solo or fronting a small ensemble, the latter of which was evident as early as her 1993 Rockquest appearance, which was executed with confidence and professionalism (Sweet As Media Limited 2008a; b). But Runga is also a multi-instrumentalist, playing guitar, which is the main instrument that has accompanied her throughout her live career, and a number of other instruments. On *Drive*, however, she plays guitar on just four tracks: 'Drive', 'Bursting Through', 'Roll Into One' and 'Heal'. Showcasing her instrumental skills, she also plays drums ('Sorry'), xylophone ('Sway', 'Hey' and 'Without You') and mellotron ('Suddenly

Strange'). Her multi-instrumental skills were evident in her 1993 Rockquest appearance at the Canterbury regional final, where Love Soup performed their song 'Superman Song' with Runga singing and playing a pair of congas and cowbell (Sweet As Media Limited 2008b). In the heat and the national final she fronted the duo, showcasing her vocal style that anticipated some of the sounds found on *Drive*, and exhibiting distinct adroitness and professionalism in her musical stagecraft.

Runga notes that in the lead-up to *Drive* she 'was writing songs in a flat in Mt Eden [Auckland] listening to a Pearl Jam record, so there was definitely all that backdrop of the '90s' (Runga, in Moses 2017). During a promotional tour of *Drive*, she noted some of her other musical influences, which included David Bowie, The Police and The Smiths (Allen 1998). Her explanation for enjoying such seasoned acts was elaborated on during an interview in the same year as the release of her second studio album. As she notes: 'Most of the musicians who really blow me away are either dead or over 50. The first time music really spoke to me was when I first heard The Smiths when I was 12' (Runga 2002). Her list of similar musical influences is extended with the likes of Neil Young, Ella Fitzgerald, Mamas and the Papas, Yoko Ono and Billie Holiday (Runga 2002).

While it is difficult to discern distinct influences from such artists in her music, in connection with *Drive*, Runga notes the sounds of the time that she can hear being inherent in the album's overall production:

I think I'm proud of how cohesive it is as an entire album, I miss working in analogue and it was made at the tail end of all-analogue album projects, before recording equipment became more affordable and people started using computers more. I like the sound of the record [*Drive*]. It has a few immature moments that I wince at, but I was very young and it really is one of those youthful break up albums that just are what they are. I can hear in the production what was around me at the time, things like U2, Grunge, Brit Pop, it was of its time but I distinctly remember trying to make something that sounded timeless, that above all that was the thing to keep in mind. (Bic Runga 2021, pers. comm.)

Regarding *Drive*'s musical style, in the lead-up to its release, Runga noted that 'it's going to be really dark because there ain't many happy songs' (Runga, in Polson 1997, 4). Her arrangements and production often offer a minimalistic musical terrain. As she comments: 'It's going to be really sparse. I write off most music I hear because it's just too busy. I like space, lots of space' (Runga, in Polson 1997, 4). A sense of space is apparent in some songs, especially in terms of the phasing in of instruments to enrich the musical texture. For example, her song, 'Bursting Through', offers such an approach, where drums are followed by the gradual inclusion of bass, guitar, voice, strings, and an increasing array of musical material. Even the re-recording of her song 'Drive' for the album offered a slightly sparser texture, especially in the guitar accompaniment.

While *Drive* is eclectic in its musical influences, Runga later had the opportunity to release an album of mostly covers, the song choice of which reflects some of the artists who inspired her musical thought. With *Close Your Eyes* (2016), while just one artist from the previously mentioned acts is included on the album (Neil Young), the covers range from the Beach Boys to Kanye West. The choice of songs is diverse, but maintains a vocal and instrumental style typical of Runga's middle-of-the-road outputs over the decades.

Closer to her own family, Runga notes that from a music performance perspective, she was initially inspired by her older sister, Boh, who had started performing in public as a teenager (Runga 2010, 52). This family connection of musical inspiration also extended to her other older sister, Pearl, as well as to her mother (see Chapter 4). Her family's musicality is also something that has influenced her songwriting process, of which she has few rules (Runga, in Allen 1998). Having little theoretical musical knowledge,[4] she notes:

> I have two older sisters who are musicians . . . but none of us is formally trained and none of us can really read music. We grew up listening to a lot of music and copied what we heard. In terms of theory, it's like being able to speak without being able to write. Then again, even if I could write it down, I don't know how many rock musicians would be able to decipher it anyway. (Runga, in Watson 1998)

In her creative work, Runga does experiment with different musical styles. As well as her EP and album versions of 'Drive', she has released several other renditions of the same song. Two very different mixes of the song are 'Drive (Doordarshan Mix)' and 'Drive (Interstellar Over Drive Mix)', both of which were included as additional tracks to Runga's fifth New Zealand single, 'Roll Into One' (1997). Both versions are electronic mixes by Tom Bailey (Thompson Twins), which move her musical

---

[4]Runga notes that she failed seventh-form (Year 13) music, commenting that 'it was nothing to do with the teacher' (Runga, in Matthews 2021).

style into uncharted territory, at least in terms of the musical style that is usually associated with the artist.

'Drive (Doordarshan Mix)' is a protracted 6'25". The track includes Runga's vocal part of 'Drive', but with this song there is a distinct Indian-sounding electronic backing that features the percussive sounds of tabla among several Indian stringed instruments. The track shows one way that a song can be transformed as a remix to achieve a very different sound to the original single (see also 'Bursting Through' and 'Sway'). Such experimentation with global sounds was not uncommon at the time, and numerous international popular music recording artists have blended the cultural sounds of the world's music with their own. Whether it's the Beatles' use of the sitar, Paul Simon's inclusion of South African music on *Graceland* (1986), or taiko drumming in the music of Imagine Dragons, with 'Drive (Doordarshan Mix)' there is a surface level of cultural influence that doesn't play out in terms of musical collaboration or distinct personal cultural roots.

A similar perspective is found with the other early remix of the song, 'Drive (Interstellar Over Drive Mix)'. At 7'16", this version of 'Drive' is an electronic mix over Runga's vocal line. This version is more of an electronic dance song with a techno sound. The track is very different to Runga's lounge style, and in contrast to her more usual sound as found on her early albums, but what the track does show, as with 'Drive (Doordarshan Mix)', is her innate predisposition to explore a wide range of musical styles.

These types of experimentation are played out later in Runga's career with her musical exploits and collaborations. For example, even when performing her early songs she sometimes preferred to use an electric guitar rather than her more usual acoustic instrument. An example of a live performance of 'Drive' helps illustrate this (see kazzart 2006). The use of an electric guitar is also found on 'Drive' in her collaborative album *Together In Concert: Live* (2000), with New Zealand music icons Tim Finn and Dave Dobbyn.

More recently, Runga has participated in other musical collaborations. She and her partner, Kody Nielson, have been active with several band line-ups. As well as appearing as Kody & Bic, the pair have worked together in electronic psych-rock bands Opossom and Silicon. Nielson also produced Runga's album *Belle* (2011a), and a remix of the song 'Drive' with Silicon as part of *Drive*'s twentieth anniversary. This further version of the song was transformational in that it was 'a complete cybernetic remodel of the classic track . . . adding vocoder vocals and Kraftwerk-style electronics while still retaining the gentle soulfulness of the original tune' (Under the Radar 2017). Runga notes her particular enthusiasm for the remix: 'It's been fun to hear "Drive" re-imagined in 2017, a song that was only ever released as an acoustic demo 20 years ago. This remix by Silicon makes me think of self driving cars and sad lovesick robots' (Under the Radar 2017).

Another band in which Runga performs is King Sweeties. This band is a collaboration between Runga (drums, engineering, production) and Cass Basil (vocals, bass) with their debut single, 'Let's Just Stay in Bed' (2020), which was produced by Nielson and has a 'modern, post punk sound' (Radio New Zealand 2020). As with her work with Opossom and Silicon, the electronic dance style of this song is quite different from the Bic Runga lounge sound that typified her musical style in the 1990s.

Runga's exploits in the sphere of 'digital reproducibility' (Babich 2018) reveal her interest in experimentation and transformative self-simulacra where successful songs such as 'Drive' are capitalized on and reproduced in a different guise, whether for personal creative expression or the commodification of a repackaged product. Related areas of her recorded outputs are found with the same songs repackaged on different releases. Taking an earlier style and finding new ways of reproducing it into a new musical sound while maintaining her vocals is at the core of her creative output. The hybrid versions of 'Drive' signify its authentic origins through the vocal line and lyrics that help in its marketability based on a recognized origin in Runga's early career. However, the reification of Runga's work exhibits an inherent contradiction in that it characterizes commodity fetishism based on 'negating the authentic' (Bloomfield 1993, 17), yet at the same time celebrating creative musical transformation through the pop music medium.

**Production.** While Runga's musical style is expressed in performance through her skills as a superb vocalist and multi-instrumentalist, it is also with the production side of her creative outputs that she excels with ardour, commitment and mastery. Within this context, Runga's overarching sonic vision stands out, not only in terms of the music product but also in the production process itself.

Runga's skills on a variety of instruments have helped her embrace the totality of creative practice. As a drummer, she was aware of the intricacies of different sounds on different types of drums, and how such sounds related to different musical styles and even musical eras:

> I had some awareness of wanting to make a sound that was timeless and I knew that the essence of that was good songwriting and also weirdly, because I was a drummer, it was to do with snare drum sounds. I think a drum sound is what dates things. (Runga, in Moses 2017)

The attention that Runga gives to the production of her music was evident early in her career during her recording work with Pagan (the four 'B-sides' on her five-track EP). During the recording sessions, Trevor Reekie observed that 'she was quite forthright about what she wanted and what she didn't want, especially about what she didn't want' (Reekie, in Moses 2017). Runga offers her own recollection of the production process, which reveals an artist with a clear direction, although constrained by inexperience in the industry. As she notes: 'I was only 18 and I didn't really know how to say no to anything. I think even back then I still knew what I wanted music-wise but I was more diffident – I didn't speak up' (Runga, in Polson 1997, 5).

At this time, the emerging teenage recording artist had a vision for how she wanted her songs to be produced, even if she had less confidence and authority to express it. The only restriction at this stage was that she was performing her songs but not producing them. The recording process for the EP showed that Runga was already embracing a large part of the performance process, but her skills actually ranged from one end of the creative process to the other, from having an idea for a song, writing it, performing it, and ensuring the recorded product actually had the sound that she wanted.

During her first recording experiences for *Drive*, Runga became disillusioned with others attempting to produce her work. She notes that she gave up on early recording sessions because she was not pleased about the direction of the recordings (Russell 1997, 20). When signed to Sony, the multinational record company sent Runga to Ireland to record, but it was because of this experience that Runga realized her desire to actually produce her own music. While the trip to Ireland was meant to offer a more fruitful result, she gave up on those sessions when working with producer Nick Seymour (Crowded House bassist) and Niall Macken. She had then been scheduled to record her debut album back in New Zealand with Dave Dobbyn, but while recovering from a car accident late in 1996, she made the decision to ask Sony if she could produce her album herself (Russell 1997, 20). As she notes: 'we had lots of failed attempts at making the record [*Drive*] and it wasn't until I took control of all the writing and production did the album finally get made' (Bic Runga 2021, pers. comm.; see also Moses 2017). However, while her recording session in Ireland didn't go the way she wanted for most of the time, the session did produce a version of 'Sway' that she was pleased with (Polson 1997, 5). Still, this version of the song, which was used in promotional recordings and as a single, was soon updated with a re-recording for the album and later single release.

In the making of *Drive*, Runga was determined to maintain creative authenticity in her songs and her performance. After all, as she notes with personal affection, they are 'fragile' (discussed later), and she was clearly a songwriter and performer who wanted to see the recorded product reflect exactly how she envisioned the songs during the writing process. As she mentioned during an interview the same year as when she released *Drive*: 'I can never understand why people would write their own music and then hand it over to someone else to produce' ('Bic Expectations' 1997).

When Runga informed Sony that she wanted to produce *Drive* herself, Sony's managing director, Michael Glading, noted: 'Her argument was, "I've tried the people you said I should try, and I believe I could do a much better job." She was so confident that she could deliver it, we had to give it a go' (Glading, in Russell 1998). It is this type of confidence, which was clearly visible in her Rockquest days fronting her duo, that combined with her musical vision to eventually enable her to convince Sony to allow her to produce her debut album.

Runga began recording and producing *Drive* in March 1997 at Revolver Studios in the suburb of Royal Oak, Auckland (Russell 1997, 20).[5] Such was her rise in the New Zealand music industry that the recording session was even mentioned in New Zealand popular music magazine *Rip It Up* ('Making Music' 1997, 31).

In connection with Runga acquiring skills and knowledge of the production process, she credits popular music luminary Peter Asher as the person who inspired her to become a producer. As she notes, for *Drive*:

I played some drums and some guitar on the record. Peter Asher was the A and R [Artists and Repertoire] at Sony NY and he had come down to Auckland and sat on the floor of my divey practice room and really empowered me to be my

[5] For the album, her song 'Drive' was recorded in Auckland at York Street Studios, and 'Suddenly Strange' at Revolver Studios and Brooklyn Recording Studios in Los Angeles. Both were re-recordings of earlier versions.

own producer. He was there for all the pre production. I credit him with teaching me what production is, he demystified the process and because the songs are fragile in their own way, balancing them with strong production was important, strong by my definition and not someone else's. (Bic Runga 2021, pers. comm.)

Runga's comments about controlling the production of the album are important in understanding her approach to the production process and the music product. Relating to the idea of creative authenticity, she recalls that even when she wrote her first song and took it to her high-school band, she thought that she no longer owned the song: 'That's when I decided that I wanted to do my own thing' (Runga 1999b). The idea of wanting to have oversight of the production was realized at high school, but not played out in practice until the recording of *Drive*, which included the early ill-fated sessions for Sony. Runga's individual and all-encompassing approach to production and product is realized on *Drive*, where she embraced every facet of the album's making: songwriting, singing, playing several instruments and producing every song on the album.

The fragility of her songs showed that Runga had an intense personal connection with her musical outputs. This intimacy was evident when recording the album, when she wanted the recording studio to have a distinct personal ambience. As she notes: 'Recording studios can be quite antiseptic places, so I recreated a home environment with lamps and rugs and things. . . . Also, most of the vocals were recorded in my home. I just took the gear from the studio home with me' (Runga, in

Gråman 2008). The idea of intimacy is important for Runga as a way of breaking the clinical aspect of recording, where a song might be broken down in numerous ways in order to attain a satisfactory production. But for the actual recording, however, Runga took the idea of intimacy back to her home, one where she was comfortable and able to record her vocals in her own time and setting.

As the album's producer, Runga was focused and very much steering the production in every way. As she notes, taking an entirely personal creative perspective: 'I really don't mind if no one likes it – you've got to make yourself happy' (Runga, in Polson 1997, 4). Not only was she strictly overseeing the recording process but her level of perfectionism is evidenced by the three weeks of intense rehearsals she put her band through before they set foot in the studio (Polson 1997, 4). But for Runga, while she maintains 'that the song is the thing' (Polson 1997, 4), in practice, it is not only the song but also with the performance and production that she exhibits mastery. As she noted in a visit to Los Angeles in 1998: 'I'm 21 and just starting and there aren't many my age who write, play and produce their own debut albums. But I like to take control and feel like it's all mine' (Runga, in Shuster 1998). In terms of the music product (i.e. the album), while having control of production, she notes that 'it was a real relief to do it myself . . . I'm roughly 100% happy with it' (Runga, in Russell 1997, 20).

In connection with Runga's role as producer, as one of her guitarists on the album comments: 'She was definite on what she didn't want. Incredible to think that she wrote, performed, called the shots and produced that album by herself at only 20'

(Thorne, in Moses 2017). As Runga clarifies: 'We had so many failed attempts, which in the end were really valuable because I learnt how to do it myself' (Runga, in McIver 1997). Runga was at the heart of the production and took the main role. As her drummer notes: 'She truly produced, steered and drove that record' (Bell, in Moses 2017). Runga took a leadership role that has been well noted by others. As one of the arrangers of 'Bursting Through' notes: 'There was no doubting who was in charge of her music and that was her' (Steven, in Moses 2017).

Reflecting the talents of the album's personnel, the songs were recorded with varying numbers of takes. For example, as one of her guitarists notes, Wayne Bell was brought in on drums and was running through 'Swim' with the band: 'we played through the song a couple of times and . . . Wayne said "how's that sounding, any thoughts?" And then Bic said "great, we've got that one. Let's do another"' (Andrew Thorne 2022, pers. comm.). Runga's vision for her songs did allow for the creative contribution of other performers on the album. For example, 'Bic's main direction for the album was that she never wanted it to "rock" but she just let everyone come up with their own parts' (Andrew Thorne 2022, pers. comm.). However, when looking at the number of takes for the vocal line, as indicated on some of the songs in the album's liner notes, Runga comments, there was intense personal reflection on what version to use: 'sometimes I'd sing 70 takes of a song, then only use bits and pieces of each of them! But I was a real novice then. Now I believe in capturing the flow of a whole take' (Bic Runga 2022, pers. comm.).

Even though Runga went through a period when she was not satisfied with the production of her songs by others, which was at the start of her professional career, she learned from such experiences and, unlike some performers, was able to assert creative authenticity over the production of her debut album.

# Case study: 'Bursting Through'

Released in 1996, 'Bursting Through' was Runga's second single, which was the preceding year to the album's release. The single, which was re-recorded with a new line-up for the album, reached No. 33 in the charts, and stayed in the New Zealand Top 50 charts for six weeks (Scapolo 2007, n.p.).

As with Runga's previous single (EP), 'Drive', the artist worked on an earlier version of the song, which was released as a single, this time with producer Karl Steven, before eventually producing her own definitive rendition for the album.[6] As she notes: 'I originally tried to record it with another producer. I didn't like how it was done. I re-recorded it and I like it now, mostly because I feel like I've reclaimed the song' (Runga 1999a). The idea of reclaiming her song from the creative vision of another producer is key to understanding the degree of artistic ownership and creative authenticity over her music that was an underpinning characteristic of Runga's emergence in the field of popular music production. After all, she was the songwriter and performer, and had a vision for what her song should sound like when made into a commercially available recording.

---

[6] For the original video with the single soundtrack, see New Zealand On Screen (1996); for the same video with the album soundtrack dubbed in, see Runga (2017a).

The main differences from the single version of the song are that the opening has a slightly different bass melody, the drum beats are less accented in the introduction, there is an absence of the guitar motif before the vocals join in and the song is fourteen seconds shorter. The overall form and instrumentation are almost identical, although there are minor differences with each arrangement.

The lyrics to 'Bursting Through' are about life and hope – in a dark room with a glimmer of light. As a main chorus line says: 'Look outside the sun it's bursting through.' Runga describes her songwriting process for the song in more detail as follows:

> I was living in a damp, dark flat by myself under someone's house and there just never seemed to be any sun. Then one day I remember this little finger of light coming through my window and it made me think, 'Oh, there is light, there is life, there is hope.' So, it was partly inspired by that little bit of sunlight and thinking about the opportunities out there. It's still a song I play live and it has this really nice finger-picking thing that I don't really know how I came up with. (Runga, in Sampson 2021)[7]

Rhythmically, the album version of the song offers a beat that drives against its common time in the vocal line. When counting in eighth notes, accented beats are given on beats

[7]While clearly about one of her experiences, the song's title also reflects Runga's own sense of bursting through and entering the world of commercial music performance. In contrast to her introspective image on her EP, in the video to accompany the single's release, she is now seen more in terms of expressing herself to the viewer (Gallagher 2012a).

1, 4 and 7, which are emphasized on the drums and bass guitar. While a slow song, these upbeat accents add a swing to the song in a similar way to many Latin music rhythms. Further, these accented beats are reminiscent of the vocal line articulation in 'Drive', her preceding single release.

The song's instruments are introduced in succession. Opening with drums and bass, the electric guitar then joins to introduce a haunting melody (not on the original single) followed by Runga's vocal line. As the guitarist notes: 'I did a delayed swell thing with a volume pedal on "Bursting Through" to compl[e]ment the string section' (Andrew Thorne 2022, pers. comm.). By the chorus, strings join in. When Runga sings the song's title line, 'Bursting Through', the drum part moves to a sixteenth-note pattern on the ride cymbal as a way of signaling the song's high point. The song's last few bars return to the minimalist drum and bass part heard in the song's introduction. The building up of layers of instruments and moments of musical tranquillity are textural devices found throughout the album, and show Runga's penchant for a minimalist sound and the building up of sonorities throughout a song.

'Bursting Through' has a verse/chorus form, but the exact length of each section is not entirely repetitive, therefore creating both predictability and unpredictability. Following a twelve-bar instrumental introduction, the overarching structure is: verse, chorus, verse, chorus, chorus, outro. With just two verses, the first is sixteen bars long, but the second is just eight bars long. While the shortening of the second verse helps move the song into its chorus, the first two choruses are each fourteen bars long. However, the third rendition of the chorus is slightly shorter, at ten bars long, which offers a shorter section while maintaining the main chorus line: 'Look outside the sun it's bursting through.' The song closes with an eight-bar instrumental.

'Bursting Through' is a ballad in Eb in 4/4 time.[8] The verse moves from tonic to dominant, and the chorus offers a harmonic exploration, particularly in the main chorus line. The first two lines of the chorus end on the dominant chord (Bb), which is resolved on Eb with the opening chord to the words 'bursting through' in the third line. After extending the harmony to C7, which resolves on Fm, the chorus ends on the dominant chord of Bb, adding an unsettled feeling to the line. This is resolved with the return to the opening of the verse on Eb. In the last line of the chorus, the Eb to Gm follows that of the verse, but the DbMaj7 extends the harmonic language momentarily before returning to the song's Eb tonal centre.

When comparing the album version of the song with Runga performing it live on vocals and guitar, the listener/viewer is able to discern in more detail the song's harmonic movement and the artist's use of the guitar (Radio New Zealand 2017). With this song, the broken (*arpeggio*) guitar chords would normally be played with a capo placed behind the third fret, which raises the overall tessitura of the song by three semitones.

# Summary

With her debut album, Runga entered the recording industry as a singer-songwriter, multi-instrumentalist and music

---

[8] Compare arrangements of the song in *Nature's Best 2* (2004) and Runga (2006).

producer. This background helped set the tone of her creative vision and saw her climb rapidly to the top of New Zealand's popular music elite. The album was toured and promoted, and Runga received numerous accolades for her musical mastery.

In making *Drive*, Runga's early musical influences gave her a language with which to explore a number of sounds, but also to create a distinctive voice that filled a niche in the New Zealand popular music market. In comparison with many other musicians, *Drive* was different for Runga. Her experiences of working with other producers led her to produce her debut album herself. Reflecting her overarching vision for the finished sound of her own music, her excursion into music production was soon recognized within the industry for its excellence. The case study of her second single, 'Bursting Through', explored her songwriting, revealing some of the detail of the song and how it paved the way to the release of her album the following year.

*Drive* is a break-up album, with dark lyrics and sparse music, each of which reflected Runga's style at the time of making the recording. Moving through the production process to create the musical product, Runga reveals the intimacy she felt with her music, and ultimately her overarching vision for how it should sound as a commercial product. A study of Runga's cultural setting in making the album, Chapter 4 explores the performer's identity (ethnicity and gender) in a country that celebrates cultural diversity within a bicultural social milieu.

# **4** Identity

## **Introduction**

Within the music industry's reception of Bic Runga and her music, the notion of identity surfaced as a factor when discussing her musical career and upbringing in Christchurch. Acknowledging the social and cultural complexities of representation, self-representation and identity politics (Bernstein 2005), most importantly, she was raised 'with an identity in music' (Webb-Liddall 2019). Runga's musical identity was certainly nurtured in a household of music making. Before moving to New Zealand, her mother (Sophia Tang) had been a professional singer in Malaysian nightclubs (Watson 1998), and Bic's sisters, Pearl and Boh, were aspiring performers ('Musical Siblings' 2016): 'There was always a lot of music around the house', she explains. 'A lot of singing. My older sisters are great musicians too and I learnt to play the guitar at 14' (Runga, in Allen 1998).[1] But musical identity was partly inspired by the gendered and cultural context that surrounded her upbringing.

This chapter discusses such influences in connection with Runga's musical identity as a distinct Kiwi icon of the

---

[1] Runga has occasionally featured her sisters on recordings or in live performances. On the album *Drive*, Boh is named as a backing vocalist on the songs 'Swim' and 'Roll Into One'.

New Zealand popular music industry. While comprehension of Runga's musical identity helps in interpreting *Drive* from a musical perspective, it is important to reflect on cultural representation and self-representation to discern some of her inspiration in the making of the album.

Runga's musical success is partly a result of her navigating identity politics within the music industry. Such matters have often been foregrounded in discourse about her music, and are discussed in this chapter as a way of investigating deeper cultural matters inherent in her music making. Recognizing the importance of being raised in a musical household, the chapter focuses on how Runga has been portrayed in the media and on her self-representation. Two distinct themes are foregrounded for discussion: ethnicity and gender. A study of each shows a distinct interconnection with her musical identity in helping motivate the artist to achieve success in an industry where gender and non-European achievement were not always recognized in equitable and unprejudiced ways. The chapter closes with a case study of Runga's song, 'Sway', which was one of her best-selling songs of the time and one that has characterized Runga's career over several decades.

# Ethnicity

The youngest of three daughters to a Malaysian Chinese mother and a Māori father (Joseph, an ex-serviceman), Runga grew up in a setting sometimes fraught with anxiety relating to Aotearoa's bicultural milieu as well as its rapidly growing multicultural ethnoscape (Ghosh and Leckie 2015). Her Kiwi upbringing in Christchurch was entangled with the notion of 'otherness' in terms of ethnic identity, but even though this included negative experiences, it helped inspire her musical artistry through self-expression in an industry dominated by white males (Millman 2021). As she comments: 'as a family, we felt quite different, I think' (Runga, in Parnell and Mohi 2021). It was this difference that sometimes featured in the media as a distinguishing element of Runga's musical brand, but also as a signifier in her self-expression.

Such 'otherness' is apparent not only in the sense of ethnicity or cultural markers of identity, which relate to her upbringing and have been particularly evident in her media representation, but also in terms of gender identity in the music business. For Runga, the hybrid context of her own cultural background, coupled with the dialectic of bicultural Aotearoa within an increasingly visible multicultural society (Ghosh and Leckie 2015), contributed to her identity in music as a voiced expression of New Zealand more broadly at the time.

In the 1990s, with growing sensitivity towards the Māori language (te reo) and Māori cultural traditions (Tikanga Māori), along with overarching Treaty of Waitangi settlement claims, Aotearoa New Zealand was beginning to reconcile a history fraught with manifest and veiled discrimination towards the nation's indigenous and other cultures (Spoonley, Pearson and Macpherson 1996). Born into a distinctly multicultural family, Runga's cultural milieu was one where cultural celebration was sometimes challenged as a result of intolerance in the wider community in which she grew up.

Runga's Māori ethnicity is a part of her identity about which she had anxieties in her childhood. In a recent interview with the UK national newspaper the *Guardian*, at a time when she and a number of other Kiwi singers were promoting te reo in the New Zealand music charts, she commented that 'it was never a good thing, a positive thing being Māori when I was growing up' (Runga, in McClure 2022). But why, for her, was being Māori at this time of her life a profound part of her identity?

She notes that when she was growing up in Christchurch there was a skinhead sub-culture, which had a racist outlook that divided communities and was intolerant of non-whites. As she comments: 'I was someone that grew up with pretty sustained, garden-variety racism' (Runga, in McClure 2022). Twenty years earlier, Runga had already mentioned racism being apparent in her home city: 'It is a very [C]aucasian city and it can be terribly racist. . . . I always felt like the token brown person. . . . There's also a real skinhead/white supremacy element' (Runga, in Pulvirenti, 2002). Her mother corroborated this by recalling Runga 'being hurt by racial taunts as a child' (Warren 2004). Even at five years old, one of Runga's teachers demanded she 'explain "what" she was' (Warren 2004). Such experiences impacted on Runga, but she comments philosophically about them: 'No country is without racism, I grew up with it, that was my experience. It has not made me bitter or ashamed. New Zealand is a beautiful and unique place' (Runga, in Warren 2004).

With a growing skinhead sub-culture in Christchurch in the 1980s, and with a resurgence in the early 1990s encouraged by the release of the skinhead movie *Romper Stomper* (Wright 1992), 'by the end of 1993 and the beginning of 1994 skinheads had started to attack and abuse mainly Asians,

Maoris and Polynesians, but also anyone else that got in their way' (Addison 1996, 103). The era in question was a time when Runga was at high school and actively nurturing her interests in popular music performance, which was when she had first-hand experiences of racism.

While speaking out against such a racist context that confronted her in her youth, a *New Zealand Herald* front-page report on a comment by Runga on the topic created debate. It noted: 'NZ a racist place, Bic Runga tells Irish paper [the *Belfast Telegraph*]' (Thomson 2004). She thought the report was very damaging (Runga, in Parnell and Mohi 2021). Such a headline is given to generate public interest and intentionally creates controversy in the way it is portrayed. But Runga had experienced racism and it was something that she has been able to comment on. For instance, as discussed later, her more recent engagement with te reo in her music is not only a concrete moment in her consolidation of her identity but also a realization of influences and encounters that have made her who she is. As she notes: 'it's kind of where my drive comes from, it's where my ambition comes from . . . to be seen as something other than just, you know, the colour of my skin' (Runga, in Parnell and Mohi 2021).

In his study of Runga's early music videos, Bannister comments that because Runga is marginalized as 'a non-white woman' in the national ethnoscape, in her music she has challenged 'dominant representations of New Zealand popular cultural identity' (Bannister 2010, 84). As a result, it has been within a largely Pākehā framework that she has crafted a musical identity that is quintessentially Kiwi (Bannister 2010, 85), which has included collaborations with established male musicians such as Tim Finn and Dave Dobbyn, who 'confer an aura of local authenticity upon her work' and confirm 'that she is symbolically "one of the boys" who can "cut it live"' (Bannister 2010, 88).

Within Aotearoa's bicultural fabric, the te reo renaissance that has surfaced over the past few decades has more recently become increasingly audible in the field of popular music. Having been suppressed for many years as a result of colonial practices, by the 1950s there were positive signs of Māori-language revitalization, albeit in a national setting still with evidence of suppression (Benton 1988, 78).[2] The revitalization of te reo gained significant traction from the 1980s with a number of new cultural measures, including kōhanga reo (early childhood language nests), kura kaupapa (Māori immersion schools) and wānanga (tertiary institutions) (Smith 1989). Such educational spaces helped nurture not only a deeper engagement with te reo, but also, for example, āhuatanga Māori (Māori tradition) and tikanga Māori (Māori custom) (Mead 2003, 11–14). Each sphere has helped forge a new era of te reo language maintenance and celebration, which has also had linguistic representation in music.

In this setting, a 2020 report by Statistics New Zealand noted that of a Māori population of 775,836, representing 16.5 per cent of the national population of 4,699,755 in 2018 ('Māori Ethnic Group' 2022), 'more than 1 in 6 Māori adults said they could speak Te reo Māori, and . . . nearly a third said they could understand the language at least fairly well'

---

[2]With English as the dominant language, Māori and New Zealand Sign Language were made official languages in 1987 and 2006 respectively.

('More than' 2020). Today, however, only about 1 per cent of the population can speak te reo fluently, and the pathway to full language revitalization has an uncertain future (Satherley 2020).

As a marker of cultural identity, the te reo sphere of linguistic expression has been voiced by Runga, both in song and sentiment. In the years since Runga was establishing her career with the release of *Drive*, New Zealand popular music has seen an increased visibility of Māori performers, and at the same time more audibility with songs in te reo. By the 2020s, the sphere of public celebration of te reo had changed with artists such as Lorde and others releasing songs successfully in the language. As Runga notes:

> If an international pop singer [i.e. Lorde] with that much reach had been singing in te reo Māori in the 80s when I was, you know, terrified, walking through the [Cathedral] square past skinheads – I would have actually felt quite a lot more security in a cultural way. (Runga, in McClure 2022)

When Runga was growing up, mainstream popular culture was almost devoid of Māori music or pop songs containing te reo lyrics. As a result of te reo revitalization and activism, in 2021, a staggering sixteen of the twenty songs in the New Zealand Singles Chart were in te reo, including songs by SIX60, Stan Walker and Paige (Trafford 2021). This form of linguistic and musical activism included international star, Lorde, releasing an EP, *Te Ao Mārama* (2021), entirely in te reo. Three of the tracks included Runga providing backing vocals. While 2021 witnessed a surge of musicians actively contributing to the te reo soundscape, the release of te reo songs was also linked to the annual Te Wiki o Te Reo Māori (Māori Language Week).

Such interest in te reo pop music was signaled several years earlier with the release of the chart-topping compilation album, *Waiata/Anthems* (2019), which comprised twelve te reo songs (re-recorded from their original English versions). The project became the annual Waiata Anthems Week, held just before Te Wiki o Te Reo Māori, which, in 2021, saw the playlist release songs by twenty-seven Kiwi performers ('Celebrating Waiata' 2021).[3] A te reo version of Runga's song 'Sway' was one of those included on the album. 'Haere Mai Rā' was the te reo title given to the song, as interpreted by translator Sir Tīmoti Kāretu, who also translated several other songs on the album. The title has the meaning 'come here' ('Bic Runga on Translating' 2019). The lyrics are not a literal translation of 'Sway', although the sentiment is as close as possible. In a postcolonial nation, Kāretu comments on the learning of te reo by non-Māori: 'if anybody's going to go to all that trouble of learning it correctly, pronouncing it correctly and wants to sing in the language, then I think it's good' (Kāretu, in McClure 2022).

Runga has shown a deep level of engagement with te reo in the recording of 'Haere Mai Rā', which is also a new arrangement of the song. Runga's Māori roots are with Ngāti Kahungunu, Rongomaiwahine (in the Māhia Peninsula in the North Island) through her father. Born into a family who didn't speak te reo at home ('Interview with Bic Runga' 2022), she is not bilingual, but a recent learner of te reo. Nevertheless, as she reflects on bringing 'Haere Mai Rā' to fruition: 'It's a really

---

[3] See https://www.waiataanthems.co.nz (accessed 3 June 2022).

profound experience . . . to sing your own language for the first time' (Runga, in Parnell and Mohi 2021). Still, the recording process was not easy and 'Runga estimates about 60 versions were recorded before she and [Hinewehi] Mohi [the producer] were happy with it, both of them determined to get all the pronunciation correct' (Webb-Liddall 2019).

Regarding Runga's Malaysian Chinese background, she notes that it was primarily her mother's musical influence that was present in the household:

> There wasn't much of a Malaysian cultural influence while I was growing up. I think her major influence is more that she used to sing around the house, and we had to practice our instruments all the time. Music is so important to her, and she has passed this down to me and to my sisters. ('Interview with Bic Runga' 2022)

It is her mother's musical influence, rather than a sense of distinct cultural tradition, that impacted on Runga's musical development. This is shown with the musical careers of all the Runga sisters. Bic Runga's exploration of te reo is one strand of her ethnicity that is played out through language, while her Malaysian Chineseness is also a signifier of her Kiwi identity, as expressed through her music more broadly.

Runga is often portrayed in terms of her 'Sino-Maori roots' ('Music' 1998a), but does this depiction relate to her music? Or is it a linguistic signifier of ethnic identity used as a marker of her perceived difference? The songs on *Drive* offer no manifest musical traits that signify distinct Māori or Malaysian Chinese traditional musical elements. However, in the contemporary world of hybrid cultural flows, Runga expresses her own identity within her music, regardless of the incorporation of sonic or cultural signifiers. Her music represents both bicultural and multicultural Aotearoa, with musical signifiers, discrete and hidden, representing a tangled Kiwi cultural identity.

# Gender

Runga's identity as a female musician has been foregrounded in many spheres of her creative work. Among a number of factors relating to her musical identity, two gender-related themes stand out and have each been featured in media reviews of her musical achievements: industry engagement and image branding. This section of the chapter discusses these themes as a way of showing not only how they are prevalent in the popular music industry but also how Runga navigated them successfully on her journey through the gendered context of her professional work. That is: How has gender been a part of Runga's industry engagement and branding? To what extent have essentialized notions of gender hindered or facilitated her career?

Within each theme, while other factors such as ethnicity and musical mastery are also present, the gendered attributes of the music industry are particularly important when considering engagement and image branding. In other words, 'the significance of . . . gender takes centre stage' (Wolfe 2018, 63), and *Drive* should be interpreted through such a lens as a way of comprehending distinct ways that Runga simultaneously (self-)essentialized the industry while de-essentializing its inherently gendered construct.

***Industry engagement.*** Runga's entry into the New Zealand professional music industry was via Rockquest. While her involvement in the competition, as well as the accolades that soon resulted, revealed gender disparities, at the same time it challenged gender stereotypes. Runga was entering a business that was dominated by men (Sisario 2018). Women had previously been involved in Rockquest, received music awards and achieved musical success, but their presence was by far outweighed by their male counterparts. This was also the case with management and other hegemonic spheres of the music industry.

Runga does acknowledge the presence of other female Kiwi singers before her. As she comments: 'when I started, there were lots of women before me – Jan Hellriegel and Fiona McDonald and Sharon O'Neill, just so many' (Runga, in Bamber 2017). However, such is the state of popular music's gender inequalities that the *New York Times* referred to it with the headline: 'Gender Diversity in the Music Industry? The Numbers Are Grim' (Sisario 2018). Between 2012 and 2017, it was revealed that of 600 songs only 22 per cent of Billboard's year-end Hot 100 chart were by women; women represented 12 per cent of songwriters; and across a subset of 300 songs, just 2 per cent of producers were women (similar figures were also found with music awards). Such figures extend to New Zealand, where similar disparities are found in music industry awards and Rockquest winners in the years around the release of *Drive*. Because of such unevenness in gender diversity in music, when a female performer achieves success, it often receives media attention in terms of its gendered creativity.

In the 1990s, Rockquest provided instructions to performers that put forward a non-gendered perspective. In 1998, for instance, its advice to contestants notes: 'DON'T TYPECAST FEMALES AS SINGERS AND KEYBOARD PLAYERS' (Rockquest 1998). While Runga was indeed a singer, she challenged stereotypical images in one band by playing drums and singing at the same time. Her mother bought her a drum kit when she was eleven, having been influenced by her older sister Boh's band ('Drive Home' 2017, 30). However, Runga did experience the gendered nature of playing drums while attending the Christchurch School of Instrumental Music (outside of high school), when boys would intervene. As she comments in connection with learning drums: 'I was really shy about it, and I'd often get pushed off them by older boys!' ('Drive Home' 2017).

Runga's entry into Rockquest in 1992 was a year that saw a recognizable presence of female vocalists fronting bands. The number was such that it was mentioned in a local newspaper, noting that six of the ten bands from Christchurch were led by women (Walker 1992, 9).[4] On clichéd perceptions of gender-based roles in popular music, the contest notes that 'gender is not relevant when determining who is capable of playing which instrument' (Rockquest 1998), yet the media still tends to foreground gender divisions. Coupled with the influence of some of her schoolteachers on feminism, such perspectives offered an environment through which Runga was able to perform in musical roles that challenged the industry's status

---

[4] Forty-four bands competed in the upper South Island heats, with fourteen in the regional final (Walker 1992, 9).

quo, and at the same time contributed excellence through performance.

Runga's career in the 1990s did not escape the dual nature of gendered creativity: artistic recognition and gendered representation. From her early years in Rockquest, she was a creative individual with songwriting and performance skills. She fronted on vocals the high-school duo that won the Christchurch regional final in 1993. From the release of her EP and debut album, her image was portrayed in the same way as most other female musicians. As discussed later, the EP portrayed a somewhat bland image, while the album offered a glammed-up image.

Runga also had another side of her identity that images could not portray. As well as leading an early band on drums and vocals, thereby contributing an instrument that traditionally has few stars, let alone singers (Smith 2014, xvi),[5] she navigated the music industry with a particularly strong female presence. She knew what she wanted in her music, which subsequently led to Sony allowing her to produce her first album, and for much of her career she has had oversight of her musical brand. With a background as a drummer, and performing drums on several tracks on *Drive* (Appendix 1), Runga not only offered difference regarding one of her chosen instruments, which helped destabilize stereotypical assumptions about gender (Berry 2016, 246), but was also under the spotlight for this very reason. Namely, while 'the drum set in popular music is perceived as a male-dominated instrument, when women

---

[5] See also *Tom Tom Magazine*, which is exclusively about female drummers: see https://tomtommag.com/ (accessed 17 May 2022).

play drums they must understand that the ways they perform on the instrument can be influenced by these discourses' (Hebert, Abramo and Smith 2017, 464).

Apart from Runga on vocals, the production of her 'Drive' EP was dominated by men. On her debut album, however, those involved in all aspects of making the album do include a female voice, but this is greatly outnumbered by men. As well as Runga, out of a team of over twenty personnel, the five female names included are Kate Walshe (violin), Sally-Anne Brown (cello), Sarah Yates (strings), Boh Runga (backing vocals) and Cindy Wilson (photography). While Runga's sister, Boh, was already achieving pop musical success, it is noteworthy that the other women involved in the album were working either in a different musical style or in photography. From management to the main instrumental backing ensemble that helped create each track, women were noticeably absent. Such gender disparity reflected the make-up of the music industry of the time, and for a female performer to offer vocal, multi-instrumental, songwriting and production skills was an achievement that both offered a strong female voice in the industry and was also a contribution that set Runga apart and promoted her musical difference.

***Image branding.*** Inherent in the popular music industry is the 'intense commodification of identities' (Negus 2017, 161). Runga's move to Sony included a change in her branding, from a self-promoting singer-songwriter performing at low-key New Zealand venues to a rising national star with major label backing working within and beyond New Zealand.

Such was Runga's presence in the New Zealand popular music scene in 1997 that a photo of her was featured on the front cover of two of New Zealand's main popular music magazines, and within a few months of each other: *New Zealand Musician* (April/May) and *Rip It Up* (July) (Figures 4.1 and 4.2). Appearing in this media just before the release of her debut

**Figure 4.1** New Zealand Musician, *April/May 1997, Auckland, New Zealand. Photo by Tony Nyberg. Hocken Collections, Uare Taoka o Hākena, University of Otago. Courtesy of NZ Musician magazine – NZMusician.co.nz.*

**Figure 4.2** Rip It Up, *July 1997, Auckland, New Zealand. Photo by Cindy Wilson. Hocken Collections, Uare Taoka o Hākena, University of Otago. Courtesy of Simon Grigg/Rip It Up Archives.*

album, the imagery helped show her elevation to the forefront of New Zealand's popular music scene. Such representations portray Runga visually, showcasing the person (i.e. her image) behind the music rather than the music itself. It is with photos like these that Runga offers a glimpse into her visual identity as part of the image branding that accompanied the release of her album, whether through ethnicity, gender or fashion. On both magazine covers, the singer-songwriter is looking straight at the camera, to the consumers of the magazine, showing a confident semblance and with her name in a large typescript that is clearly visible and a reminder of who she is.

On the *Rip It Up* cover, Runga's name is printed in three colours (foregrounded in orange with a white and black outline) and runs across her body as a distinct textual expression. Taken by Cindy Wilson, the same photographer for her album cover, the photo depicts Runga sitting cross-legged in a corner.[6] Her make-up and hair are the same as on the album cover, but her clothing is different: on the magazine wearing a white fur jacket and torn-at-the-knee blue jeans. In the article that accompanies the *Rip It Up* feature, Russell (1997) provides insight into Runga's rapid rise to the upper echelon of New Zealand music and the image she aimed to control. As Runga comments: 'things like photo shoots, videos and interviews are largely out of your hands. But when it comes to the music, it's important to maintain control' (Runga, in Watson 1998). Her comments about controlling her music lie at the heart of her creative pursuits, which is to maintain her own expressive vision for her music. Even though she recognized that her media image is staged as part of her branding, as on the front covers of *New Zealand Musician* and *Rip It Up*, she

---

[6] Further photos from the same photoshoot were put up on Runga's website. See https://web.archive.org/web/19990827160336fw_/http://www.bicrunga .com/index.html (accessed 7 April 2022).

did insist on having a veto over marketing strategies (Russell 1997, 21). As she notes: 'the last thing I want to be seen as is a record company product' (Runga, in Russell 1997, 21). Further, as Reekie comments, when recording with her in 1994, 'nothing was going to phase her . . . it was her who was going to drive' (Trevor Reekie 2022, pers. comm.). It is with such a perspective that Runga makes music at a juncture between creative authenticity and commercial product (Moore 2002; Moorefield 2005; Zagorski-Thomas 2014), where the contested processes of maintaining artistic control and the need for industry branding create a contradictory tension she is keen to balance.

The album cover of *Drive* depicts Runga to the right of the sleeve with her name and the album title displayed on the left. Set on a light blue background, Runga's name is given in capital letters, helping to capture the attention of a viewer, and the name of the album is written using what appears to be her handwriting (when compared with the hand-written titles and lyrics that feature in the liner notes). Unlike her EP, the album uses her performing name, Bic Runga, adding her Māori family name and localizing her to Aotearoa. The use of handwriting for the album's title, and throughout the liner notes with song lyrics, offers a personal element that is easily contrasted with a typeface intended for mass use. Such an individual touch helps to signify a sense of intimacy, one that is reflected in Runga's songs and performance style, which is characterized by voice and instrumental (often guitar) accompaniment. This visual form of textual communication is often found in marketing, such as when companies write a personal letter to a customer using (electronic) handwriting in order to attempt a 'human-to-human' approach (Kotler, Kartajaya and Hooi 2017, 99).

The main album cover features a near full-length picture of Runga. She is in a corner, as on the *Rip It Up* cover, but this time a ceiling corner rather than the floor. Dressed in a short green dress and wearing a long blue coat with a black fur collar, the performer sports heavy black eyeliner and eye shadow (harmonizing with the colour of her hair and coat collar) with her head leaning slightly to one side and eyes looking directly at the camera (the consumer). Her stance is noticeably different to her EP cover in that, with the album, she is facing her audience, offering a more confident outlook and with more glamorous attire. Such bodily positioning helps symbolize a friendly and welcoming performer. That is, on first meeting someone, which in this case is the consumer seeing the album cover, direct eye contact and a slight head tilt are clear welcoming signals that have a positive impact on the person being greeted (Phipps 2012, 74, 185).

Regarding her clothing on the album cover, Runga notes:

My sister [Pearl] had made the green dress for me and the jacket was just from a thrift [charity] store. I think I might've done my own hair and makeup and I remember the main role models for me as a woman of colour would've come from R and B music videos that I'd grown up watching. I do remember at the time there was nowhere that sold make up for someone my colour. I remember that being a problem for quite some time but I'm glad that's all changed now! And that pop culture seems more diverse than it was back then. (Bic Runga 2021, pers. comm.; see also Runga, in Moses 2017)

Her costuming appeared to be a personal expression – how Runga wanted to be presented, and what was available to her at the time – rather than a totally staged photo shoot with supplied costumes and a make-up artist. It is here that Runga still shows personal authenticity over her image, one that also reflected her overseeing of *Drive*'s production. As she confirms: 'It wasn't like someone styled my clothes or anything. It felt quite comfortably me. There's sort of varying degrees of awkwardness at photo shoots, but that wasn't one of the worst ones' (Runga, in Moses 2017). At the time of making the album, Runga noted further detail about how she liked to appear:

> I try not to make it a game of dressing up. I don't like to be styled. If I had my way, I'd wear something simple. The thing is, people still want to know how you look. It's like music videos. They don't have as much soul as songwriting. I find making them tedious and tiring. And usually, they're the producer's vision. (Runga, in Taib 1997)

It is here that Runga reveals her desire to maintain her authenticity with her public image: not too staged, and allowing people to see who she really is.

The liner notes of *Drive* have several further iconographic elements that help in interpreting Runga's music industry branding, musical aspects and song meaning. The lyrics to 'Drive' are depicted with a superimposed 'turn right' road marking, therefore offering a literal meaning of the song that connects it to driving a vehicle. This road theme, which signifies the album's title, is also found elsewhere in the liner notes, either showing white road markings or with Runga looking out of a car window. There are two further pictures of

Runga: one showing her legs on a staircase, and the other lying on a bed. These pictures of the artist offer a sense of female identity while adding elements of sensuality. With a sense of incongruity, another photo depicts food. A musical aspect is added to the lyrics of 'Roll Into One' as depicted with the song's time signature (4/4) and chord symbols.

After the New Zealand release of *Drive*, and as part of her promotional tour for the album's international release in 1998, Runga associated herself with the increased visibility of women singer-songwriters. In a music scene with a growing number of such performers (Dix 2005, 280), Runga had entered the international professional music scene at a time that helped foreground her identity. She featured on two album releases of women musicians that had been initiated during her US promotional tour in 1998 (Various Artists 1998; 1999). At that time, 'women singer-songwriters who had been steadily ploughing a furrow through the early 90s finally reached critical mass' (O'Brien 2012, 375). Runga was unquestionably part of this movement, and her association with Lilith Fair (see Chapter 5) reflects international recognition by her peers. But this sphere of popular music was also aligned to commercialism in that 'by the late 90s, female songwriters had emerged, blinking, from the underground to become a major commercial phenomenon' (O'Brien 2012, 377).

Runga reflects much on her gender identity within the music industry. Even when *Drive* was released she questioned her female place in music. As she comments: 'On my more cynical days I wonder whether I would have been signed if I were a boy, because it's quite fashionable to be a female singer/songwriter' (Runga, in McIver 1997). It is with such a comment that Runga acknowledges the inherent androcentrism of the music industry and shows a degree of uncertainty over her musical skills and female presence. It is also with such a comment that Runga reinforces her focus as a singer-songwriter as the core aspect of her public image, regardless of how she is (self-)portrayed in the media.

But Runga's engagement with issues around gender identity is deeper than media reflection, and personal, albeit within a distinct national perspective. Reflecting on her female identity, she comments:

> I think of feminism in NZ as a unique national experience. We were the first country to give women the vote. This uniqueness can be attributed to Māori women of the 1890s, already land owners, looking for enfranchisement and so partnering with the European Suffragette movement. This has given feminism here its own flavour. All my high-school teachers were very strong second wave feminists and it wasn't until I left school and left the country did I realise that there was still a long way to go for women in terms of equality. But it was drummed into me early on, and that's partly why I thought it was perfectly ok to fight for my own songwriting and production, it seemed obvious to me even though it wasn't common to produce yourself or write your own songs, certainly not when working with major labels. There was that feeling of being a product or a creation that I had to learn to reject and [speak] . . . up against, but it was really hard at the time. (Bic Runga 2021, pers. comm.)

Runga clearly locates her female voice within a national setting. She acknowledges the gendered New Zealand landscape as unique, noting specific historical moments in women's rights. In this context, she was also inspired by her education, where she was influenced by feminist thought, although only on leaving New Zealand was she able to reflect deeply on these experiences. Such aspects are important in helping to explain how and why she sought to produce her debut album, and also shed light on some of her (feminist) motivations as a female singer-songwriter whose talents challenged stereotypical roles in the music industry in maintaining her gendered creative control and agency (Boak 2016, 257), while simultaneously being marketed as a product of the music scene. In this context, 'she is now firmly ensconced as part [of] our national *taonga* [treasure], pioneering a pathway for a younger generation of talented and outspoken female vocalists like Lorde, Anika Moa, Anna Coddington, and Ria Hall. Long may she drive' (Davis 2017).

# Case study: 'Sway'

'Sway' (1997) was Runga's third single and was re-recorded for the album.[7] In terms of the song's musical style, Runga

---

[7] As with 'Drive' and 'Bursting Through', there are several slightly different versions of 'Sway' and its video (Gallagher 2012b; New Zealand On Screen 1997; Savage 2017). For the video to the single version not on the album, see Runga (2014); for the video to the album's track and later single, see dublin75 (2007). In addition to these versions of the song, which are very similar, Runga has also recorded several others, including a live performance (Runga, Finn and Dobbyn 2000), an acoustic voice and guitar track branded as 'even better than her original version' (Various Artists 2004), and the Lilith Fair acoustic version, which unlike other versions of the song, has a melancholic minor chord at the end of one chorus line: 'Instilling so much doubt it makes me' (Various Artists 1999). Further, while Gary Verberne played most of the guitar parts on the album with Andrew Thorne playing the solo, when touring the album, Thorne drew on an earlier version of the solo: 'It turned out there's a

comments that 'it's really pillowy and warm and analogue' (Runga, in Moses 2017). With such reflection, one can realize the type of sound that was at the core of Runga's musical vision. That is, she seemed to strive towards an authentic sound with minimal intervention in the production.

Runga reveals several influences on the song. These include elements from John Lennon and Ella Fitzgerald, which are noted in contrasting ways and both surreptitiously:

> I think Sway was an attempt at a John Lennon song, that sort of semitone warble of the b section [3rd verse] 'now it all turns sour', that's almost a borrowed nuance of his, but it's not that overt. I found lots of places to warble my way through otherwise quite simple songs, I was trying to find my own vocal style. My favourite singer is Ella Fitzgerald but you wouldn't hear that influence especially either, but she was a dancer and I think her phrasing is especially lightfooted and swingy, like she's dancing. (Bic Runga 2021, pers. comm.)

With 'Sway', Runga was further exploring her song style. The song contrasts with her two previous singles, which offered more of a vocal style without overt vibrato and softer in style and instrumentation. 'Sway' on the other hand had a stronger beat and pop music aesthetic.

The idea for the title was from graffiti Runga had seen on her way to Auckland Airport in New Zealand (Runga 1999a).

---

nice guitar line that was on the original "Sway" recording which never made the album – I ended up playing that part live because people seemed to miss it' (Andrew Thorne 2022, pers. comm.).

Offering further knowledge about her visual and sonic inspiration, she continues:

> I wrote that on my porch, and again it just happened really quickly: it seemed to write itself. People might already know this but there was a piece of graffiti on the Wellesley Street bridge which said 'sway'. I just liked the word and the image it conjured up. I'd also been listening to David Bowie a lot and there's that great line in 'Let's Dance' where he sings 'sway through the crowds to an empty place', so that word just resonated with me. (Runga, in Sampson 2021)

'Sway' is essentially about love:

> Songs like 'Sway' are about how full of contradictions being in love is. How can a thing make you happy but also make you sick? How can it make you feel strong one minute and then powerless and stupid the next? It's such an adolescent record. (Runga, in 'Drive Home' 2017)

Runga is often inspired by street scenes in everyday life. As she notes: 'I remember wondering what had driven someone to go to all the effort of climbing up there to write that word ["sway"]. I'm often inspired by things like that – street signs, shop signs, words you just see as you're walking around' (Runga, in Allen 1998). Regarding her lyrics, she notes: 'My songs are not exactly autobiographical, but they are inspired by things that I come across – say something I see as I'm walking down the street' (Runga, in Allen 1998).

The song went on to be one of Runga's hits, achieving gold status and acknowledged with various accolades at the New Zealand Music Awards. Its path to success was helped with the song (the album version) featuring during several love scenes towards the end of the movie *American Pie* (1999) (Runga, in Moses 2017), which provided her with further international attention.

The musical structure of 'Sway' reveals insight into Runga's songwriting process. Acknowledging that her reflection on the song over two decades later may reveal a critical element, she notes:

> I really took songwriting seriously, almost as a job. I remember writing Sway and kind of thinking it was a bit cringey but I put it on the pile of songs nonetheless, as part of a day's work. I had no idea that song would become the most popular, I really don't think it's my best song. (Bic Runga 2021, pers. comm.)

'Sway' extends Runga's singer-songwriter-guitarist style into a band line-up with guitars, bass and drums. Adding to this, strings are included with violin and cello, along with Runga contributing backing vocals and xylophone. The song is in 4/4 time in the key of A. 'Sway' has a verse-chorus form, although closer analysis reveals several structural deviations that add dissimilitude and avoid absolute uniformity:

Intro – 4 bars
Verse – 12 bars ('A', 'A', 'B')
Verse – 12 bars
Chorus – 8 bars
Verse – 12 bars
Chorus – 16 bars
Bridge – 4 bars

Solo – 4 bars
Verse ('B' section) – 8 bars
Chorus – 16 bars
Outro – 8 bars

After the third verse, the chorus is played twice, offering an extended reinforcement of the song's main lyric, which consists of two key lines: 'Say you'll stay . . . Sway my way'. The repeated chorus is followed by a four-bar bridge that leads to a four-bar guitar solo. But it is following this vocal repose that the song's structure takes another form, one that adds a sense of familiarity yet at the same time offers further variation. Here, rather than going into another entire verse, or even a chorus, Runga offers the four-bar 'B' section of the verse twice, forcibly anticipating the return of the chorus. As expected, the chorus returns, again played twice, and is followed by an outro that repeats material from the bridge.

With this structural foundation, 'Sway' has harmonic material with relatively few chords, but occasionally with moments of dissonance and ambiguity. The instrumental introduction moves from chords IV to V, which provides a cadential formula leading to the first verse:

> Above, the lead guitar plays the melodic line A-G#-A in each bar. The harmonic analysis of these four bars reads IV-V-IV-V because there seems little point in complicating the simple progression with IVsus#4 and Vsus4 chords that only last for a single quaver. (Braae 2012, 65)[8]

---

[8] Compare the arrangement in Runga (2006).

The verse's harmony progresses A, C#m, D, D, which is repeated although ending with E in place of D in the previous line. The verse closes with a section that adds a new chord, F#m, followed by C#m, D, E leading to the chorus. As with the introduction, this adds weight to the beginning of the chorus, which comprises A, E, F#m, C#m, E. While using a relatively simple harmonic language, the bridge and solo offer a layering of harmonic ambivalence with different melodic motifs on voice and guitar over a guitar and bass backing.

# Summary

Identity for Runga is multifaceted. There are overlapping spheres of meaning that help her showcase her songs through Runga the brand. But this brand is a person, one whose often intimate lyrics and music reflect the self, a personal expression shared through commercial music yet articulated in a distinctly individual way. Relating to her identities, Runga summarizes how she represents people, whether marginalized groups or female artists, and such engagement has had an impact not only on those who consume her music but also on the artist herself:

> I'm meeting people in their 20s now [whose] . . . parents would put that album on in their family cars, or when their babies were falling asleep. It was the biggest selling NZ album at the time so at one point it was everywhere. I'm really humbled by this, that what was just an obsession and a struggle for me, just became part of other people's daily lives. I'm proud of all of the fight, especially where I feel like I represent marginalised groups. This is still where I find comfort and strength and I have

met many female artists in NZ who tell me it made them feel like they could make music too. (Bic Runga 2021, pers. comm.)

This chapter has explored two themes relating to Bic Runga's identity: ethnicity and gender. Each has been influential in helping the artist craft her music and make her who she is. Regarding ethnicity, this has been foregrounded in media reviews of Runga's music, but has also been an aspect of her Kiwi identity with Māori culture being an increasingly important facet in her life. She's a Kiwi, and, as she comments: 'Both my cultures are important to me, but it's hard to differentiate between those cultural influences and the things I just am as a person' (Runga, in Allen 1998).

Runga's gender identity has played out in her industry engagement in several ways. Working in a male-dominated field, her early move into production was unusual at the time, and a process that she navigated with authority and control. These traits also related to her image branding, where she strived to maintain the authenticity of her product. With the release of *Drive*, Runga had a rapidly growing presence in New Zealand popular music, which is reflected in the media publicity of her work. 'Sway' was one of Runga's biggest hits, and the short case study helped show detail about its background and musical form, each of which offers insight into the songwriter's creative process.

# 5 Performance

## Introduction

Live performance for Bic Runga has been a central part of her career, especially in terms of profile raising activities and album promotion. This was particularly the case around the mid-1990s, when she emerged as a shining light in New Zealand popular music. Focusing on her promotional touring of *Drive*, including the lead-up to the album's release in 1997 and its international release the following year, this chapter explores Runga's performance activities in New Zealand and overseas. Following the release of her 'Drive' EP in 1995, the main period in question started in 1996 with the launch of her single 'Bursting Through', which was followed by the single 'Sway' in 1997 before the release of her album the same year. These were an intense few years for Runga, which extended to 1999 as she continued to promote her album internationally.

The purpose of this chapter is to follow the performance processes that Runga experienced as a result of *Drive*, from growing a fan base locally to international performances across four continents. The discussion is taken further by exploring Runga's local and international touring in light of her identity and creative authenticity. Touring in New Zealand helped consolidate Runga's identity as a Kiwi musician with a diverse cultural background, and in an international setting strengthened her distinct cultural brand. Such promotional activities, while growing her image and commercial attraction, seemed to function in opposition to the idea of ownership that underpinned her production process. That is, notwithstanding the creative elements of performance, promotional touring had an unmistakable element of mass commercialism, a process that was part of Runga's popular music identity, yet it moved her away from the musically creative aspects of her song production and the oversight she strived to maintain. The last two New Zealand singles released from the album, 'Suddenly Strange' and 'Roll Into One', are included as short case studies to help further illustrate key points concerning Runga's creative process.

## National scene

With the release of two singles and a debut album in the planning, Runga was set to embark on a promotional tour of New Zealand that would help pave the way for her album release in mid-1997, thereby raising her profile and potential album sales. However, her initial plans for touring were postponed because of an injury sustained as a result of a car accident in late 1996, although she was back on the stage in early 1997 promoting her music.

Runga's first major appearance in 1997 was when she performed at the Big Day Out music festival in Auckland on 17 January, which was held in Ericsson Stadium.[1] This event was

---

[1] The 'Big Day Out' music festival had its origins in Australia in 1992 and included New Zealand in the years 1994–7, 1999–2012 and 2014. At its height,

particularly significant in terms of its size and artist association of over forty acts with whom Runga would be appearing. With an audience of 31,000, which was massive for a New Zealand music festival, and an array of local and international acts (Cole 1997), she was billed as 'Bic Runga & Band', pointing to her move to group performance and away from her singer/guitarist profile.[2] As she noted the year before, 'I want to get away from that sort of acoustic thing and have more of a band sound' (Runga, in NZ On Air 1996). The inclusion of backing musicians also helped pave the way to her recording session for *Drive*, which would soon follow and include an array of instrumentalists. Runga's appearance at the Big Day Out was early recognition of her standing in New Zealand music, which was based on the relative success of her 'Drive' EP and 'Bursting Through' single.

Once the recording for *Drive* was finished, Runga was soon on the road again promoting her first album in the media and through performance. At the time, she commented on the speed at which her career was developing, especially in terms of the promotional aspects that are an inherent component of being a pop music performer. As she noted: 'After the last day mixing the album, it's been full-on press ever since. . . . It seems so strange. There are songs on this album which I wrote two years ago, and now things are going so quickly' ('Driving Straight to the Top' 1997). Her perspective of moving fast within the music industry helps show the impact of the marketing process on her: selling music to a consumer audience in a context of mass production,

---

the festival was held in five Australian cities and in Auckland, New Zealand (Cummings 2007).
[2] Runga's older sister, Boh, was performing with her own band (stellar*) at the same event.

distribution and consumption. It is here that Runga was not only writing, recording and producing her songs, but also part of a media brand that necessitated artist and album promotion, including live performances and other marketing media such as interviews and photo shoots, which moved her creative authenticity into a commercial sphere governed by sales.

The importance of Runga promoting her music to a live audience relates to the idea of building a larger fan base of potential consumers. While in the 1980s and 1990s music video was rapidly developing as a further tool for music promotion (Frith 1988b), the importance of establishing a public performance profile in New Zealand was still a primary part of the industry, which reflects the lack of dedicated TV music channels at the time, and in a national context with limited music agencies and performance opportunities. As Paul Ellis, promotions manager at Sony Music New Zealand, commented in the early 1990s: 'It is now a standard practice that most record companies, whether they be multi-national or independent, are shying away from signing an artist or a group which has no live profile' (Ellis, in Shuker and Pickering 1994, 264). In this context, while Runga had already gained a New Zealand following, she had now entered the sphere of large-scale music promotion with the aim of increasing sales of her commercial brand. While she was rapidly increasing her New Zealand fan base through live performance, which complemented her single releases, she would soon be applying this marketing model overseas and to a potentially much larger consumer market.

At this time, Runga was being prepared by Sony for an international career in addition to her increasing popularity in

New Zealand. Runga's entry into the popular music industry followed the typical model developed in the 1960s, which involved working in a relatively low-key music scene to build up a local following, and then moving to regional work and indie recording to expand the fan base (Frith 1988a). This process is ideally followed by a recording contract and international touring. The cycle consists of 'creating and working-up new musical material for performance, studio recording and touring, and once again back to creating and recording to keep the momentum going' (Shuker 2001, 111). Runga had now entered this cycle, and her New Zealand promotional work was to lead the way for the international release of her music (singles and album).

Following the release of *Drive*, by August 1997 Runga's promotional work for her album was moving ahead at full force. She was already advertising gigs across New Zealand in September: in Dunedin, Queenstown, Wellington, Hamilton and Auckland ('Tours' 1997a, 6; b, 6). In the popular music magazine *Rip It Up*, her debut album was given a page-length promotion that included a photo of the album cover and another promotional photo of the artist, thereby showcasing the person behind the music through branding imagery. The wording in the advertisement stressed that the album featured her three singles to date (not noting they were new versions of the singles already released): 'Sway', 'Drive' and 'Bursting Through'. The singles weren't listed in chronological order, but in order of popularity: No. 7, No. 10 and No. 33 in the New Zealand Top 50 charts, respectively (Scapolo 2007, n.p.). A review of the album by Martin Bell was also featured in the same issue, where he reminded readers of Runga's string of accolades to date, and noted that her 'star seems destined to continue its meteoric rise', which it certainly did (Bell 1997).

Soon after the release of *Drive*, Runga's extensive promotional performances were noted in October 1997 in a regional New Zealand newspaper article:

> BIC RUNGA takes her seat at Palmerston North Airport just minutes before the boarding call for her flight back to Auckland on Sunday. She had been in the city for less than 12 hours to play a brief show at the International Pacific College open day before returning home to prepare for a month-long tour of Australia and Asia. Runga then goes on to America, where she will promote her album, Drive, briefly and shoot a video. 'And then back here for a New Zealand tour in December – it's a lot of work, but I'm looking forward to it,' she said. ('Bic Runga Strikes' 1997)

Over just a few months, Runga was traveling extensively in New Zealand and overseas, covering three continents, with the aim of promoting her album through live performances and media publicity. While this short period may have seemed intense for a relative newcomer to the music industry, her relentless promotional work for the album continued into the following year.

By the end of 1997, her touring schedule in New Zealand was expanded to include eighteen gigs over December and January, and coinciding with the release of a further single, 'Roll Into One', thereby capitalizing on single releases in addition to the album.[3] The tour was promoted by CRS Music Management

---

[3] Consolidating her increased commercial engagement with the music industry, Runga registered her company, Bric Music Ltd, in January 1998. See https://app.companiesoffice.govt.nz/co/891491 (accessed 11 April 2022).

as her 'Drive Summer Tour '97/98' ('Bic Runga: Drive Summer Tour' 1997, 13; 'Tours' 1997c). These performances, which Runga performed with her band, included New Zealand's main urban centres as well as some smaller venues such as the Waihi Beach Hotel and the Coroglen Tavern in Whitianga. The size of such venues helped Runga further expand her potential fan base in a way typical of music industry promotion (Shuker 2001, 109). The diversity of the venues helps show Runga's appeal to a range of fans, as well as how her music was promoted as far and wide as possible across the nation as a way of capitalizing on her recent rise to national stardom.

The mix of being signed to a multinational label and performing extensively in New Zealand with the backing of a management company confirmed Runga's entry to the upper echelon of the New Zealand music industry.[4] From here, Runga was to branch out internationally as part of a commercial move intended to capitalize on her New Zealand popularity and attempt to emulate and build on this beyond the national setting and thereby aim to further commodify her music with potential for increased financial gain.

## International scene

New Zealand has produced a number of popular music artists and bands that have achieved international success (Brunt and Stahl 2018, 2). Bic Runga is one such performer, whose

[4]Based on Shute's (2018) analysis of Spotify data, in 2018, Runga was still a popular New Zealand singer, placed seventeenth in a list of monthly worldwide Spotify streams of New Zealand artists.

career in the international music scene has included single and album releases and performances in many countries.

Runga's promotion of *Drive* was enduring, and from 1997 to 1999 she 'played over 200 performances around the world . . . sometimes solo acoustic (as on the 1998 Lilith Fair tour across the USA) and other times with a full backing band' (Runga 1999b). The fluctuation of backing musicians reflected her ability to perform solo as a singer-guitarist or fronting a band.

Runga pursued her career under the management of Campbell Smith, who was later to become her brother-in-law when he married her sister, Boh. The support of such management helped move Runga into the international music scene. With the release of *Drive* in the United States in mid-1998, Smith's involvement was an essential ingredient in promoting her music to a wider audience. Their collaboration was one of mutual benefit that aimed to increase her profile and subsequently music sales:

> They were both fresh. She was an international priority artist for Columbia/Sony and he dealt with labels, publishers, booking agents, promoters and the rest. [As Smith said:] 'With a group, their closest relationships are generally with each other. But Bic and I spent two years travelling the world together. It's a constant relationship and not an altogether always comfortable one. You're often all the other person has'. (Brown 2013)

With much more work involved, Smith helped craft Runga's career in a commercial way where she was promoted as a prospective star with the backing of a major record label.

For some of the first part of 1998, Runga was based in New York to promote her music to a potential US market and to use this East Coast base as a strategic point for travel to Europe for further promotional performances (Watson 1998):

> Since February [1998], Runga has been flitting between New York, London and major cities in Europe, doing promotional work. It is unlikely she will return to New Zealand till at least the middle of the year. 'Bic's in good spirits and holding up very well despite all the travel,' Smith says. 'She's enjoying seeing the world and doing the work. We are really happy, primarily because so many countries have put their hands up and said they want to release the album, which is a hard thing in itself'. (Alexander 1998)

Runga notes that there is a degree of compromise when promoting her music: between the creative artist and the commercial product. This included not living in New Zealand in 1998. As she comments: 'I didn't really choose New York myself but the album's coming out in America, so I have to plug away at playing live and doing Press' (Runga, in Watson 1998). With such a comment, the impact of the commercial side of music promotion is very clear. Performing and media promotion were essential parts of breaking into a larger consumer market.

With this base, Runga's time in the United States involved a number of performances at diverse venues and across distant locations. In April 1998, she was performing on the East Coast of the United States, with appearances at well-known venues such as the Kendall Cafe in Cambridge, Massachusetts (Sullivan 1998). She offers insight into her thoughts on being at the centre of a promotional campaign. 'It's not a real life, though; it's very make believe. . . . I guess it's a suitcase kind of thing. What's difficult is the other side of this industry where you have to do the grinning and smooching and the handshaking and dining' (Runga, in Cooper 1998). It is with such a comment that one realizes that Runga as a commodity is incongruous with her creative vision. The relentless promotional touring of *Drive* from 1997 to 1999 was not only something new to her in the international sphere but also a work-related activity demanded by the music industry and requiring endurance.

As well as her US appearances, Runga performed in Europe, traveling to London in 1998, which included gigs at well-known London venues: the Borderline in April, and at the Monarch in June ('Music' 1998a; b). With these performances, she was promoted on both occasions in terms of her ethnicity with 'Sino-Maori roots', as well as the success of her debut album in New Zealand. Such marketing offered a dual way of perceiving the artist by association and without hearing her music. The mention of her mixed ethnicity adds a degree of cultural branding that would fit well in the world music market where ethnicity is often foregrounded in the promotion of music to western audiences. The hybridity of Malaysian Chinese and Māori ethnicity offered Asian and indigenous cultural signifiers with a sense of difference to a UK audience. As well as these cultural associations, the success of *Drive* in New Zealand is referred to as a marketing tool that acknowledges the album's reception outside of the UK, thereby inferring a preconceived degree of excellence. This was a process of adding value as a brand identity (Donham 2015): Runga being promoted in terms of her mixed ethnicity and as a proven Kiwi musical commodity.

The extent of Runga's touring is seen with her appearances in North America, Europe and Australia. By mid-1998, she was performing in Australia, supporting Kiwi music legend Neil Finn on tour (Cooper 1998; Watson 1998). Such an appearance also feeds into brand identity. In this case, there was a reciprocal relationship between Finn and Runga. Finn was connecting with an emerging artist, one with whom he would later collaborate on recordings, and Runga was associating herself with an established artist and thereby strengthening her position as a credible performer.

Runga performed at the Arts Centre, Melbourne, on 9 July 1998. Just two days after, she was performing at the music venue, Dingwalls, at Camden Lock, London ('Rock & Pop Music' 1998), and the next month at the New World Music Theatre, Illinois, United States, on 5 August. As part of her August tour in the United States, she also performed at the Metro Cafe in Washington, DC (Jenkins 1998), and at the well-known food and music venue Wilbert's Bar & Grille, in Cleveland, Ohio (Scott 1998). The scope of her performances included an array of smaller venues as shown with an appearance at Starbucks Coffee in Cleveland Heights in Ohio (Scott 1998). Starbucks was a sponsor of the Lilith Fair traveling festival of women performers and produced a CD available at the store, *Lilith Fair '98: A Starbucks Blend CD* (Various Artists 1998), which included 'Sway' (Traiman 1998).[5] Later in 1998, Runga performed at the

---

[5] Lilith Fair releases also included Bic Runga on Various Artists (1999) with an acoustic version of 'Sway' (see Chapter 4).

Colorado Music Hall as the opening act for alternative band Better Than Ezra, where her 'clear, powerful and exquisitely phrased' voice received an enthusiastic response from one reviewer (Johnston 1998). Runga showed her suitability for larger events by appearing in Cincinnati at the traveling music festival Lilith Fair (Simmons 1998). Soon after, she was further promoting her album in the UK, which included an appearance on the TV programme, *Soundtrax*, on Carlton TV on 17 September 1998 ('Thursday' 1998).

After her numerous international performances, Runga returned home to New Zealand in early 1999. Reflecting on her touring experiences while promoting *Drive* to an international audience, she commented: 'I was so driven and naive when I started out, I'd never even been overseas before. I thought the music industry was going to be exciting and magical, but I realised it's mostly about marketing and sales figures' (Runga, in Pulvirenti 2002). It is with such a statement that tension is revealed between Runga the creative artist working in the popular music industry and her experiences as a commercial product of the industry. She recognized that popular music was about sales, and that to increase sales the artist needed to promote the brand.

The impact of international touring allowed Runga to broaden her experience of global cultures. As she notes: 'I got to see the world, I think I'd had a pretty sheltered existence up until then' (Bic Runga 2021, pers. comm.). Even though other Kiwi musicians have broken into the international market, often via Australia (Giuffre 2018, 207), the need to travel extensively is usually an inherent component for achieving commercial success.

Runga points out the relative geographic isolation of the Kiwi music industry. Her 'sheltered existence', while a personal perspective open to interpretation, might also be taken as a national phenomenon that is played out more broadly in the New Zealand music industry in terms of the nation's relatively small consumer market and the enticement of performers to travel overseas to a larger consumer base. In connection with Australia, which might be compared geographically to New Zealand in terms of its location far removed from its former colonial homeland, Blainey (1966) has referred to a 'tyranny of distance' that has helped shape history. In connection with popular music, Brunt and Stahl (2018, 5–8) contextualize this trope in the Australasian setting in relation to Anderson's notion of 'imagined communities' (1983), where 'the notion of distance resonates and inflects how popular music mediates fundamental sociospatial relationships' (Brunt and Stahl 2018, 6). For Runga, touring overseas was not only an essential part of her growth into a lucrative commercial music market, and an industry expectation connected to being signed to a multinational record label, but it also offered her a way of broadening her cultural knowledge beyond New Zealand.

While much of Runga's promotional work was in the United States and Europe, with the release of *Drive* and the impact it was making in South East Asia, Runga made several promotional visits to this region in November 1997: 'The album has already been picked up by most south-east Asian territories, with Runga making hit-and-run promotional visits to Kuala Lumpur, Singapore and Hong Kong last month' (Alexander 1997). However, reflecting on her break into the international music industry, at the end of November, she was already traveling further afield, in 'Los Angeles . . . working with director Josh Paft (Stone Temple Pilots, Pearl Jam) on a new video for Sway' (Alexander 1997). This was followed by a three-week break, and then further work in the United States to promote her album (Alexander 1997).

Runga's grueling performance schedule continued into 1999. She played at the Big Day Out for the second time in January 1999, thereby consolidating her national and international success with a major homecoming performance. This was followed by a short New Zealand tour, before heading back to the northern hemisphere in March that year for further international performances (Armstrong 1998).

# Case studies: 'Suddenly Strange' and 'Roll Into One'

The last two singles to be released from *Drive* in New Zealand were 'Suddenly Strange' and 'Roll Into One'.

**'Suddenly Strange'.** 'Suddenly Strange' was Runga's fourth single, which was released in 1997 after the album's release.[6] As a single, which entered the New Zealand Top 50 charts in late September 1997, it wasn't as successful as her previous singles, reaching No. 26 and staying in the charts for five weeks (Scapolo 2007, n.p.). The song is about a relationship break-up with one partner trying to leave the other (Runga, in Allen 1998). As the last line of the chorus says: 'I suppose it's over now.'

---

[6]For the video of the song, see Runga (2017b).

The song opens with Runga on voice and guitar in the first verse. Melodic accompaniment joins the second half of the second verse with a four-note pattern with the first note rising by a semitone each time (E, A, C, E / F, A, C, E / F#, A, C, E). The texture later thickens with the inclusion of further instruments: bass, drums, hand percussion, mellotron, strings and backing vocals. When writing the song, Runga was inspired by the Beatles' use of strings, which she wanted to imitate (Runga 1999a). Another connection with a Beatles' sound (e.g. 'Strawberry Fields Forever') is with the inclusion of a mellotron.

The song is in 4/4 time with a G tonal centre with the last line of both the verse and chorus ending on the dominant chord D. The verses progress along the following underlying harmonic structure: G F Em E Am Fmaj7 Am D (Runga 2006). The use of a bVII (F) follows a similar harmonic movement in popular music with this chord offering a modal sound and a substitute for the dominant chord. A further element of harmonic development is with the chord progression Em to E, with the latter functioning as V of ii and momentarily moving the harmony to a secondary dominant before ending the line on the dominant chord (D).

The song's structure follows a form typical in outline of much popular music:

Verse: 8 bars
Verse: 8 bars
Chorus: 8 bars
Verse: 8 bars
Chorus: 8 bars
Instrumental/Verse: 10 bars
Chorus: 8 bars
Instrumental/Ending: 24 bars

The instrumental section before the last chorus reveals a distinctly skillful form, where a short instrumental interlude, which is a climactic point in the song, is seamlessly joined over ten bars (as opposed to the eight-bar sections in previous verses and choruses) to a closing verse.

**'Roll Into One'.** 'Roll Into One' was Runga's fifth single and released in 1997.[7] The song entered the New Zealand Top 50 charts on 19 December 1997 and peaked at No. 48 (Scapolo 2007, n.p.). Offering a country feel on guitar, the song also features Boh Runga on backing vocals. As a single, and showing Runga's approval of remixes, the two other tracks on the single are alternative versions of 'Drive': 'Drive (Doordarshan Mix)' and 'Drive (Interstellar Over Drive Mix)' (see Chapter 3).

'Roll Into One' is about wishful thinking about a possible relationship. As one line says: 'If I could make you mine.' The lyrics mention sitting out in the sun and the summer rolling by. As Runga notes: 'I call it my Cliff Richard song. I find it quite comic because it's exceedingly sweet' (Runga 1999a). Her reference to Cliff Richard reflects some of her early musical influences from listening to her parents' music, which also included an early appreciation of Shirley Bassey and the Carpenters (Mills and Howells 2020).

The song is in G, with the harmonic movement from F to G (bVII–I) at the end of each verse and chorus offering a cadential ending found in much popular music. Each line consists of eight bars in 4/4 time, except for the outro, which is extended

---

[7] The song was also released with a video directed by Paul Casserly. See https://www.youtube.com/watch?v=2B3-TJ5qmhA (accessed 14 April 2022).

through repetition. *Drive*'s liner notes include a hand-written summary of the chords used for the verse and chorus:

| Verse | C | G | C | G |
|---|---|---|---|---|
| | Am | G | F | G |
| Chorus | Am | Em | Am | Em |
| | F | G | F | G |

The introduction has the full band with lead guitar providing a melodic reverb sound with a distinct country feel. But the band falls silent with the opening verse except for steady drums and Runga's vocals.[8] The guitar enters only in the last two bars. The second verse follows a similar style, but with the guitar providing more fills throughout. By the first chorus the band offers more backing, which develops further as the song progresses, especially by the second chorus with the inclusion of backing vocals. An eight-bar instrumental is a chance for the lead guitar to develop a solo, which is layered on top of a slightly different harmonic structure.

# Summary

This chapter has introduced some of Runga's performances during her *Drive* era. Leading up to the album's release, and following through with promotional performances for the

---

[8]See also her live video of the song for voice and guitar, which confirms her vision for the underlying harmony: https://www.youtube.com/watch?v=8M_aAAJgPsw (accessed 14 April 2022).

next few years, the artist undertook a grueling time on the road, both nationally and internationally.

Working initially with smaller audiences in the national scene, Runga followed the typical music industry model and built up a substantial fan base. Following the success of her EP, she embarked on promoting her forthcoming album. With a rapidly growing presence in the music scene, Runga was soon contracted to Sony and her career took off, which included much promotional work across four continents.

The short case study of 'Suddenly Strange' helps show some features of Runga's songwriting, arranging, performance and production. The case study of 'Roll Into One' introduced Runga's last single from her album. While not as successful as her earlier singles, the study of the song showed her exploration of harmony, song structure and musical style, each of which combines to showcase her skills in songwriting and production.

# **6** Conclusion

Bic Runga's *Drive* was a landmark album for the rising star of New Zealand popular music. As her debut album release, *Drive* showcased Runga's musical abilities in several ways, including as a songwriter, multi-instrumentalist and producer. The album represented Runga as a musician as she entered the national and international spheres of the commercial popular music industry. Her songs stood for her identity as a Kiwi, expressing the social and cultural milieu of her individual imagination through the creative sounds of her music. *Drive* was an assemblage of Runga's making, with its denouement being her impressive layer of music production, which offered a sense of creative authenticity that heightened the album's allure and, ultimately, firmly placed her en route to the New Zealand Music Hall of Fame.

In this book, Chapter 1 provided a succinct introduction to the relevance of studying *Drive* in the context of popular music studies. Runga's rise to national stardom was initiated with her self-produced *Drive*, which led to many music industry accolades across the spectrum of album creation. Continuing her distinctive career in music, she was inducted into the New Zealand Music Hall of Fame as an established Kiwi musician who had contributed songs for over two decades that were a part of the lives of many New Zealanders. While this short biographical information can only offer a glimpse into Runga's life and career, what it does capture is the significance of her early years in the professional industry as the pivotal point for her ultimate success in the upper echelon of New Zealand music.

Chapter 2 outlined Runga's performance activities in connection with her breaking into a professional career soon after leaving school. Her high-school years performing in bands and in Rockquest were fertile ground for nurturing a life working in music. In these bands, she was not only a member but a leader through her vocal mastery, and, in one band, she also led playing drums. Her participation in Rockquest gave her performance experience and inspiration to achieve in a competitive environment where female drummers were not a common feature. Runga's break occurred as a result of several intersecting circumstances, and over just a few years after she left school: she gained national recognition as a runner-up in Rockquest in a pop music duo, she released a commercial EP that received chart success, her musical skills were acknowledged by music industry peers with various accolades and she ultimately self-produced her debut album under a contract with a major multinational record label.

Runga's route to the New Zealand Music Hall of Fame may have been initiated by *Drive*, but the artist also released more music in the years following *Drive*, much of which has continued the success set in motion by her highly acclaimed debut album. In Chapter 3, a closer look at *Drive* showed that her musical oeuvre had production at its core. As a break-up album, *Drive* offered a dark and sparse sound that is characterized by Runga's distinctive voice within a minimalist soundscape of varied musical styles. But one key strand that stands out on the album is Runga's music production, which, while being a commercial product, also has a sense of musical intimacy in terms of Runga's sensitivity towards her vision for the final sounds of her songs. This sense of musical identity is reinforced by her re-recording several songs for the album that had already been released as singles, therefore expressing a distinct authenticity through her creative sonic imagination.

The discussion in Chapter 4 emphasized Runga's identity and creative authenticity in the making of *Drive*, illustrating Runga's artistry across multiple spheres of album conception. Runga's identity can be understood across several areas, including musical, gender, cultural and national. Each of these elements has made Runga who she is and thereby helped the artist create her music as an expression of her personal musical imagination. For much of her career, Runga's ethnicity and gender have been markers of her identity, as portrayed in the media, whether in concert promotion or reviews, identifying her as between cultures but still an emblem of Kiwi music. The idea of gender is central to Runga's motivation in creating music, presenting a female voice as a music producer, as a drummer (among other instruments) and as an icon of the New Zealand music industry. Such factors of identity construction helped Runga offer a sense of creative authenticity in her production of *Drive*. Her various roles allowed her to maintain artistic control over her music and produce the sounds she wanted for the album. Her musical vision offered authenticity, which was a factor that contributed to her musical appeal.

With the release of *Drive*, both nationally and internationally, Runga pursued a grueling schedule of album promotion that spanned several years. As discussed in Chapter 5, entering the music industry as a local artist, with *Drive*, and contracted to Sony, she was to travel far and wide in a quest to promote her music within and beyond New Zealand. At home, and acknowledging her contribution to Kiwi music, Runga continued to receive music industry accolades, and her international performance schedule helped consolidate her wider artistic recognition in New Zealand.

Five case studies of songs are included in the book. These short studies help showcase some of the features of the New Zealand singles that were released leading up to or from the album. The songs vary in their musical style, and the studies show Runga's songwriting skills in a variety of ways but she maintained her lead vocals throughout. Writing in a pop music idiom, she explores song structure, harmonic elements, musical style and instrumentation. Rock sounds are juxtaposed with those from country, strings are blended with pop, and solo performing is contrasted with band work. The singles received differing degrees of public reception in terms of sales. There were slightly different versions of some of them produced for the album, as well as the inclusion of non-album songs on some singles. However, while such a commercial aspect of her music industry work is dominated by unit sales, she skillfully steered a route within popular music that is a commercial product on the one hand, yet revealed creative authenticity on the other.

*Drive* helped propel Bic Runga to national stardom. As she notes: 'I'm happy to be the youngest person in the NZ Music Hall of Fame, even though with that it feels like my career is all in the past' (Bic Runga 2021, pers. comm.). However, she continues, 'I still have music in me and I'm still as obsessed by production and songwriting as I ever was. But it is a very different time now. I don't know what it must be like to be starting out in music now' (Bic Runga 2021, pers. comm.). From this perspective, *Drive* is an album representative of a Kiwi icon, a recording that showcases identity and creative authenticity, and a product that epitomizes an artist's musical expression and vision at a significant juncture in her emerging musical career.

# References

'All Keyed up for Rock Quest' (1989), *Christchurch Star*, 3 August: 10.

'Bic Expectations' (1997), *Sunday Mail*, 23 November: 29.

'Bic Runga: Drive Summer Tour '97/98' (1997), *Rip It Up*, December: 13.

'Bic Runga on Translating "Sway" Into Te Reo' (2019), Radio New Zealand, 14 September. Available online: https://www.rnz.co.nz/national/programmes/nat-music/audio/2018713191/bic-runga-on-translating-sway-into-te-reo (accessed 27 April 2022).

'Bic Runga Strikes It Big with First Album Hit' (1997), *The Evening Standard*, 22 October: 16.

'Celebrating Waiata Anthems Week 2021' (2021), Sony Music, 3 September. Available online: https://www.sonymusic.co.nz/celebrating-waiata-anthems-week-2021/ (accessed 21 February 2022).

'Drive Home' (2017), *Cityscape*, 28 September. Available online: https://cityscape-christchurch.co.nz/blog/whats-on/entry/drive-home (accessed 11 April 2022).

'Driving Straight to the Top' (1997), *Evening Post*, 18 September: 25.

'Infocus – Smokefree Rockquest' (1993), NZ On Screen. Available online: https://www.nzonscreen.com/title/in-focus-smokefree-rockquest-1993 (accessed 28 March 2022).

'Interview with Bic Runga' (2022), Hawkes Bay Arts Festival 2022. Available online: https://www.hbaf.co.nz/festival-stories/bic/ (accessed 11 April 2022).

'Listen: Bic Runga – Close Your Eyes' (2016), *Under The Radar*, 17 October. Available online: https://www.undertheradar .co.nz/news/11743/Listen-Bic-Runga---Close-Your-Eyes.utr (accessed 28 March 2022).

'Making Music: Rumours' (1997), *Rip It Up*, April: 31.

'Māori Ethnic Group' (2022), Statistics New Zealand. Available online: https://www.stats.govt.nz/tools/2018-census-ethnic -group-summaries/m%C4%81ori (accessed 21 February 2022).

'More than 1 in 6 Māori People Speak Te Reo Māori' (2020), Statistics New Zealand, 9 November. Available online: https:// www.stats.govt.nz/news/more-than-1-in-6-maori-people -speak-te-reo-maori (accessed 21 February 2022).

'Music' (1998a), *Times* (UK), *Metro*, 25 April: 33.

'Music' (1998b), *Times* (UK), *Metro*, 6 June: 33.

'Musical Siblings – Bic, Boh, and Pearl Runga' (2016), From the Weekend with Emile Donovan, 9:40 a.m., 16 January. Radio New Zealand. Available online: https://www.rnz.co .nz/national/programmes/the-weekend/audio/201785672 /musical-siblings-bic,-boh,-and-pearl-runga (accessed 23 February 2022).

'Rock & Pop Music' (1998), *Guardian* (UK), 11 July: D45.

'Smokefreerockquest 2013–25 Years of Music Success: The History – with Founders and Directors Pete Rainey & Glenn Common' (n.d.), Smokefree Rockquest. Available online: https://smokefreerockquest.co.nz/wp-content/uploads/2018 /02/SFRQ-history-Rainey-Common.doc (accessed 3 February 2021).

'Thursday' (1998), *Times* (UK), 12 September: 24.

'Tours' (1997a), *Rip It Up*, August: 6.

'Tours' (1997b), *Rip It Up*, September: 6.

'Tours' (1997c), *Rip It Up*, December: 8.

'Trevor Reekie' (2021), Radio New Zealand. Available online: https://www.rnz.co.nz/national/presenters/trevor-reekie (accessed 2 January 2021).

Addison, R. (1996), 'Alienation and Skinheads: An Exploratory Study into the Attitudes of an Antisocial Subgroup of Society', MA diss., University of Canterbury, New Zealand.

Alexander, M. (1997), 'Runga's Career Ready to Move into Overdrive Overseas', *Sunday News* (Auckland), 7 December: 20.

Alexander, M. (1998), 'Bic's Year', *Sunday News* (Auckland), 19 April: 29.

Allen, V. (1998), 'Bic in New Zealand', *Scotland on Sunday*, 26 July: S12.

Anderson, B. (1983), *Imagined Communities: Reflections on the Origin and Spread of Nationalism*, London: Verso.

Aotearoa Music Awards (2020). Available online: https://aotearoamusicawards.nz/ (accessed 18 January 2022).

APRA AMCOS (2022), 'Silver Scroll Award'. Available online: https://www.apraamcos.co.nz/music-creators/awards/silver-scroll-awards (accessed 23 March 2022).

Armstrong, A. (1998), 'Runga Books Chch Concert', *The Press* (NZ), 24 December: 17.

Arts Online (2021a), 'Coke Smokefree Rockquest 2003'. Available online: https://artsonline.tki.org.nz/Teaching-and-Learning/Secondary-teaching-resources/Music-Sound-Arts/Reviewed-resources/Key-Collection/Coke%20Smokefree%20Rockquest%202003 (accessed 1 January 2021).

Arts Online (2021b), 'History of the Rockquest'. Available online: https://artsonline.tki.org.nz/Teaching-and-Learning/Secondary-teaching-resources/Music-Sound-Arts/Reviewed-resources/Key-Collection/Coke%20Smokefree%20Rockquest%202003/History%20of%20the%20Rockquest (accessed 1 January 2021).

Babich, B. (2018), 'Musical "Covers" and the Culture Industry: From Antiquity to the Age of Digital Reproducibility', *Research in Phenomenology*, 48: 385–407.

Bamber, S. (2017), 'Beautiful Collision: A Conversation between Bic Runga and Brooke Fraser', Stuff, 29 January. Available online: https://www.stuff.co.nz/entertainment/music /88728875/beautiful-collision-a-conversation-between-bic -runga-and-brooke-fraser (accessed 7 June 2022).

Bannister, M. (2010), '"Going out to Everyone"? Bic Runga as a "New Zealand" Artist', in H. Johnson (ed.), *Many Voices: Music and National Identity in Aotearoa/New Zealand*, 84–9, Newcastle upon Tyne: Cambridge Scholars Publishing.

Bell, M. (1997), 'Bic Runga: Drive', *Rip It Up*, August: 27.

Benton, R. (1988), 'The Maori Language in New Zealand Education', *Language, Culture and Curriculum*, 1 (2): 75–83.

Bernstein, M. (2005), 'Identity Politics', *Annual Review of Sociology*, 31: 47–74.

Berry, M. (2016), 'Gender Identity, the Queer Gaze, and Female Singer-songwriters', in K. Williams and J. Williams (eds), *The Cambridge Companion to the Singer-songwriter*, 246–56, Cambridge: Cambridge University Press.

Blainey, G. (1966), *The Tyranny of Distance: How Distance Shaped Australia's History*, Melbourne: Sun Books.

Bloomfield, T. (1993), 'Resisting Songs: Negative Dialectics in Pop', *Popular Music*, 12 (1): 13–31.

Boak, S. (2016), 'The Female Singer-songwriter in the 1990s', in K. Williams and J. Williams (eds) *The Cambridge Companion to the Singer-songwriter*, 257–64, Cambridge: Cambridge University Press.

Braae, N. (2012), 'A Musicological Analysis of *Nature's Best*', MA diss., University of Waikato, New Zealand.

Brown, R. (2013), 'Campbell Smith Is Back in the Ring', *Metro*,
29 November. Available online: https://www.metromag.co.nz/
arts/arts-music/campbell-smith-is-back-in-the-ring (accessed
17 March 2022).

Brunt, S. and G. Stahl (2018), 'Introduction: This Is My City:
Reimagining Popular Music Down Under', in S. Brunt and
G. Stahl (eds), *Made in Australia and Aotearoa/New Zealand:
Studies in Popular Music*, 1–16, New York: Routledge.

Clayton-Lea, T. (2004), 'Glamorous and Glitzy? Don't Look at Me',
*Irish Times*, 15 March: 12.

Cole, B. (1997), 'Huge Party for Music Masses', *Daily News* (NZ),
20 January: 2.

Cooper, S. (1998), 'This Bic's Not Disposable', *Sydney Morning
Herald*, 3 July: 7.

Cummings, J. (2007), 'Sold Out! An Ethnographic Study of
Australian Indie Music Festivals', PhD diss., University of
Western Sydney, Australia.

Davis, H. (2017), 'Bic Runga Celebrates the 20th Anniversary of
*Drive*', *Scoop*, 6 November. Available online: https://www
.scoop.co.nz/stories/CU1711/S00078/bic-runga-celebrates
-the-20th-anniversary-of-drive.htm (accessed 11 April 2022).

Dix, J. (2005), *Stranded in Paradise: New Zealand Rock and Roll,
1955 to the Modern Era*, rev. edn, Auckland: Penguin Books.

Donham, T. (2015), 'The Value of Branding in the Music
Business', in A. Macy, C. Rolston, P. Allen and T. Hutchison,
*Record Label Marketing: How Music Companies Brand and
Market Artists in the Digital Era*, 3rd edn, 83–106, New York:
Routledge.

Frith, S. (1988a), *Music for Pleasure: Essays in the Sociology of Pop*,
Cambridge: Polity Press.

Frith, S. (1988b), 'Video Pop: Picking Up The Pieces', in S. Frith (ed.),
*Facing the Music*, 88–130, New York: Pantheon Books.

Gallagher, R. (2012a), 'Bic Runga "Bursting Through"', 5000 Ways to Love You: Exploring the World of NZ On Air Music Video Funding, 22 March. Available online: https://5000ways.co.nz/1996/april-1996/bic-runga-bursting-through/ (accessed 18 January 2022).

Gallagher, R. (2012b), 'Bic Runga "Sway"', 5000 Ways to Love You: Exploring the World of NZ On Air Music Video Funding, 23 February. Available online: https://5000ways.co.nz/1997/february-1997/bic-runga-sway/ (accessed 18 January 2022).

Gallagher, R. (2013), 'Love Soup "You"', 5000 Ways to Love You: Exploring the World of NZ On Air Music Video Funding, 5 September. Available online: https://5000ways.co.nz/1994/december-1994/love-soup-you/ (accessed 18 January 2022).

Ghosh, G. and J. Leckie, eds (2015), *Asians and the New Multiculturalism in Aotearoa New Zealand*, Dunedin: Otago University Press.

Giuffre, L. (2018), 'Negotiating Trans-Tasman Musical Identities: Conversations with Neil and Tim Finn', in G. Stahl and S. Brunt (eds), *Made in Australia and Aotearoa/New Zealand: Studies in Popular Music*, 207–17, London: Routledge.

Gråman, S. (2008), 'Bic Runga: The Star of Tomorrow'. Available online: http://www.graman.net/bic/ (accessed 1 March 2022).

Grigg, S. (2022), 'Lost Record Stores of Inner Auckland', AudioCulture, 16 March. Available online: https://www.audioculture.co.nz/articles/lost-record-stores-of-inner-auckland (accessed 21 April 2022).

Hall, S. (1996), 'Introduction: Who Needs "Identity"?', in S. Hall and P. du Gay (eds), *Questions of Cultural Identity*, 1–17, London: Sage Publications.

Hayward, P., T. Mitchell and R. Shuker (1994), 'Preface', in P. Hayward, T. Mitchell and R. Shuker (eds), *North Meets South*:

*Popular Music in Aotearoa/New Zealand*, i, Sydney: Perfect Beat Publications.

Hebert, D., J. Abramo and G. Smith (2017), 'Epistemological and Sociological Issues in Popular Music Education', in G. Smith, Z. Moir, M. Brennan, S. Rambarran and P. Kirkman (eds), *The Routledge Research Companion to Popular Music Education*, 451–78, New York: Routledge.

Jenkins, M. (1998), 'Bic Runga "Drive" Columbia', *Washington Post*, 31 July: N12.

Johnson, H., ed. (2010), *Many Voices: Music and National Identity in Aotearoa/New Zealand*, Newcastle upon Tyne: Cambridge Scholars Publishing.

Johnston, K. (1998), 'Better Than Ezra's Antics Mix Fun with Great Vocals', *The Gazette* (Colorado Springs), 7 December: LIFE 8.

Keam, G. and T. Mitchell, eds (2011), *Home, Land and Sea: Situating Music in Aotearoa New Zealand*, Auckland: Pearson Education New Zealand.

Kennedy, B. and D. McCrum (2020), 'Interview with Wayne Bell', Podcast: Don't Give Up Your Day Job, 85. Available online: https://ndhadeliver.natlib.govt.nz/delivery/Deliver yManagerServlet?dps_pid=IE64053373 (accessed 5 June 2022).

Kotler, P., H. Kartajaya and Hooi, D. H. (2017), *Marketing for Competitiveness: Asia to the World! In the Age of Digital Consumers*, Hackensack: World Scientific.

Long, P. and S. Barber (2017), 'Conceptualizing Creativity and Strategy in the Work of Professional Songwriters', *Popular Music and Society*, 40 (5): 556–72.

Machin, D. (2010), *Analysing Popular Music: Image, Sound, Text*, London: Sage.

Matthews, P. (2021), '1999: Bic Goes Back to School', *The Press* (NZ), 8 May: B2.

McClure, T. (2022), 'From Outrage to No 1 Hits: How Māori Musicians Conquered the Charts in Their Own Language', *Guardian* (UK), 4 February. Available online: https://www .theguardian.com/world/2022/feb/05/from-outrage-to-no -1-hits-how-maori-musicians-conquered-the-charts-in-their -own-language (accessed 23 February 2022).

McIver, S. (1997), 'Drive Time', *The Press* (NZ), 25 July: 21.

Mead, H. M. (2003), *Tikanga Māori: Living by Māori Values*, Wellington: Huia.

Millman, E. (2021), 'Here's How White and Male the Execs of the Music Business Are', *Rolling Stone*. https://www.rollingstone .com/pro/news/music-industry-executive-diversity-usc -1184000/ (accessed 27 April 2022).

Mills, A. and R. Howells (2020), 'Bic Runga Profile', AudioCulture, 6 November. Available online: https://www.audioculture.co.nz /people/bic-runga (accessed 2 January 2021).

Moore, A. (2002), 'Authenticity as Authentication', *Popular Music*, 21 (2): 209–23.

Moorefield, V. (2005), *The Producer as Composer: Shaping the Sounds of Popular Music*, Cambridge, MA: MIT Press.

Moses, H. (2017), '"Just Let Her Do the Album by Herself": An Oral History of Bic Runga's Drive', *The Spinoff*, 17 October. Available online: https://thespinoff.co.nz/music/17-10-2017/just-let-her -do-the-album-by-herself-an-oral-history-of-bic-rungas-drive (accessed 20 January 2022).

*Nature's Best: New Zealand's Top 30 Songs of All-Time* (2002), Roseberry, N.S.W.: Wise Publications.

*Nature's Best 2: More of New Zealand's Top Songs of All-Time* (2004), Roseberry, N.S.W.: Wise Publications.

Negus, K. (2017), 'The Gendered Narratives of Nobodies and Somebodies in the Popular Music Economy', in S. Hawkins (ed.), *The Routledge Research Companion to Popular Music and Gender*, 152–65, New York: Routledge.

New Zealand On Screen (2021), 'Love Soup'. Available online: https://www.nzonscreen.com/title/love-soup/artist (accessed 28 January 2021).

Nowak, R. and S. Baker (2018), 'Popular Music Halls of Fame as Institutions of Cultural Heritage', in S. Baker, C. Strong, L. Istvandity and Z. Cantillon (eds), *The Routledge Companion to Popular Music History and Heritage*, 283–93, New York: Routledge.

O'Brien, L. (2012), *She Bop: The Definitive History of Women in Popular Music*, rev. 3rd edn, London: Jawbone Press.

Pekacz, J., ed. (2006), *Musical Biography: Towards New Paradigms*, Aldershot: Ashgate.

Phipps, R. (2012), *Body Language: It's What You Don't Say that Matters*, Chichester: Capstone.

Polson, A. (1997), 'Bic Runga: Getting the Bic Idea', *New Zealand Musician*, 6 (8): 4–5.

Pulvirenti, A. (2002), 'Artist MOST Likely', *Sunday Herald* (Melbourne), 15 September: Z16.

*Review of Copyright Act 1994* (2019), New Zealand Music Industry Submission: Response to MBIE Issues Paper.

Roach, M. (2015), 'New Zealand Music Awards 1973–2014', AudioCulture, 4 November. Available online: https://www.audioculture.co.nz/articles/new-zealand-music-awards-1973-2014 (accessed 21 March 2022).

Rockquest (1998), 'Getting Your Group Together', 13 June. Available online: https://web.archive.org/web/19980613220827/http://www.rockquest.xtra.co.nz/booklet/28get.html (accessed 7 April 2022).

Runga, B. (1998), 'Bic Runga', 13 June. Available online: https://web.archive.org/web/19980613220629/http://www.rockquest.xtra.co.nz/booklet/20bic.html (accessed 7 April 2022).

Runga, B. (1999a), 'Bic Runga Talks about the Songs on Drive', 8 May. Available online: https://web.archive.org/web/19990508224822/http://www.bicrunga.com/music.html (accessed 28 February 2022).

Runga, B. (1999b), 'Bic Runga Biography', 10 December. Available online: https://web.archive.org/web/20001213111000fw_/http://www.bicrunga.com/bio.html (accessed 1 March 2022).

Runga, B. (2002), 'Bio', 12 August. Available online: https://web.archive.org/web/20020805063946fw_/http://www.bicrunga.com/bio01.html (accessed 17 May 2022).

Runga, B. (2006), *Bic Runga Songbook*, Taren Point: Alfred Publishing Australia.

Runga, B. (2010), 'Bic Runga', in I. Chapman, *Kiwi Rock Chicks, Pop Stars & Trailblazers*, 50–3, Auckland: HarperCollins.

Russell, J. (1997), 'Fit to Burst: Bic Runga', *Rip It Up*, July: 20–1.

Russell, J. (1998), 'New Zealand's Bic Runga "Drives" Sony Debut to Top', *Billboard*, 28 February: 14, 91.

Sampson, D. (2021), 'Bic Runga on Bic Runga, 2012', AudioCulture, 13 August. Available online: https://www.audioculture.co.nz/articles/bic-runga-on-bic-runga-2012 (accessed 12 April 2022). Originally published in *Rip It Up*, February/March 2012.

Satherley, D. (2020), 'Māori Language Likely Doomed, Despite Recent Uptick in Speakers – Study', *Newshub*, 10 January. Available online: https://calendar.google.com/calendar/u/0/r/week?tab=qc (accessed 21 February 2022).

Savage, S. (2017), 'Talking "Sway" with Bic Runga'. Available online: https://www.vice.com/en/article/vv57bj/talking-sway-with-bic-runga1 (accessed 26 April 2022).

Scapolo, D., comp. (2007), *The Complete New Zealand Music Charts, 1966–2006: Singles, Albums, DVDs, Compilations*, Wellington: Maurienne House.

Scott, J. (1998), 'Cooper Has New Snake, and the Boa Must Go On', *The Plain Dealer*, 31 July: 20.

Shuker, R. (1994), 'Climbing the Rock: The New Zealand Music Industry', in P. Hayward, T. Mitchell and R. Shuker (eds), *North Meets South: Popular Music in Aotearoa/New Zealand*, 16–27, Sydney: Perfect Beat Publications.

Shuker, R. (2001), *Understanding Popular Music*, 2nd edn, London: Routledge.

Shuker, R. (2005), *Popular Music: The Key Concepts*, 2nd edn, New York: Routledge.

Shuker, R. (2008), 'New Zealand Popular Music, Government Policy, and Cultural Identity', *Popular Music*, 27 (2): 271–87.

Shuker, R. and M. Pickering (1994), 'Kiwi Rock: Popular Music and Cultural Identity in New Zealand', *Popular Music*, 13 (3): 261–78.

Shuster, F. (1998), 'Pop/Sneak Peek New Zealand Sensation Bic Crafts Her Signature Debut', *Daily News* (Los Angeles), 1 May: 22.

Shute, G. (2018), 'By the Numbers: The New Zealand Music with the Most Spotify Streams', *The Spinoff*, 19 February. Available online: https://thespinoff.co.nz/music/19-02-2018/by-the -numbers-whats-the-most-streamed-new-zealand-music (accessed 17 January 2022).

Simmons, C. (1998), 'Sound Check', *Dayton Daily News*, 22 May: 19.

Sisario, B. (2018), 'Gender Diversity in the Music Industry? The Numbers Are Grim', *New York Times*, 25 January. Available online: https://www.nytimes.com/2018/01/25/arts/music/ music-industry-gender-study-women-artists-producers.html (accessed 6 April 2022).

Smith, A. (2014), *Women Drummers: A History from Rock and Jazz to Blues and Country*, New York: Rowman & Littlefield.

Smith, L. T. (1989), 'Te Reo Maori: Maori Language and the Struggle to Survive', *Access: Contemporary Issues in Education*, 8 (1): 3–9.

Songfacts (2021), 'Drive by Bic Runga'. Available online: https://www.songfacts.com/facts/bic-runga/drive (accessed 24 January 2021).

Spoonley, P., D. Pearson and C. Macpherson, eds (1996), *Nga Patai: Racism and Ethnicity in Aotearoa/New Zealand*, Palmerston North: Dunmore Press.

Sullivan, J. (1998), 'A New Zealand Surprise', *Boston Globe*, 2 April: 30.

Sweet As Media Limited (2008a), '4. Rockquest 1993 Canterbury Regional Final: Part Three 2 of 2', 17 September. Available online: https://www.youtube.com/watch?v=iS_ZkAqXf8A (accessed 22 March 2022).

Sweet As Media Limited (2008b), '9. Rockquest 1993 Canterbury Regional Final: Part 7 2 of 2', 19 September. Available online: https://www.youtube.com/watch?v=dE7KrVdEJio (accessed 22 March 2022).

Sweetman, S. (2012), *On Song: Stories behind New Zealand's Pop Classics*, Auckland: Penguin Books.

Taib, S. (1997), 'Storming up the Charts with Bic Runga', *New Straits Times*, 25 November: 5.

Thomson, A. (2004), 'NZ a Racist Place, Bic Runga Tells Irish Paper', *New Zealand Herald*, 29 March. Available online: https://www.nzherald.co.nz/nz/nz-a-racist-place-bic-runga-tells-irish-paper/7Z3AMO6UD6VYUZPODVTNIDQW34/ (accessed 16 June 2022).

Trafford, W. (2021), 'Te Reo Māori Dominates NZ Music Charts', *Te Ao*, 24 September. Available online: https://www.teaomaori.news/te-reo-maori-dominates-nz-music-charts (accessed 21 February 2022).

Traiman, S. (1998), 'Starbucks, Lilith Link With CD, Cafe', *Billboard*, 4 July: 1, 95.

Under The Radar (2017), 'Premiere: Silicon Remixes Bic Runga's "Drive"', *Under The Radar*. Available online: https://www .undertheradar.co.nz/news/13255/Premiere-Silicon-Remixes -Bic-Rungas-Drive.utr (accessed 28 January 2021).

Walker, B. (1992), 'Women Upfront in School Bands', *Christchurch Star*, 19 August: 1 (photo), 9. Available online: https://discoverywall.nz/ album/1540/1720 (accessed 25 February 2022).

Warren, A. (2004), 'Irish Racism Reports Upset Singer', *The Press* (NZ), 30 March: A2.

Watson, C. (1998), 'Driven Bic Steers Her Own Course', *Central Coast Herald*, 4 July: 18.

Webb-Liddall, A. (2019), 'Bic Runga on Finding Her Voice in Te Reo Māori: "It's Invigorated My Whole Life"', *The Spinoff*, 11 September. Available online: https://thespinoff.co.nz/atea/11 -09-2019/bic-runga-on-finding-her-voice-in-te-reo-maori-its -invigorated-my-whole-life (accessed 22 February 2022).

Wolfe, P. (2018), '"An Indestructible Sound": Locating Gender in Genres Using Different Music Production Approaches', in S. Bennett and E. Bates (eds), *Critical Approaches to the Production of Music and Sound*, 62–77, New York: Bloomsbury Academic.

Zagorski-Thomas, S. (2014), *The Musicology of Record Production*, Cambridge: Cambridge University Press.

Zwaan, K. and J. de Bruin, eds (2012), *Adapting Idols: Authenticity, Identity and Performance in a Global Television Format*, New York: Routledge.

# Discography/Videography

dublin75 (2007), 'Bic Runga – Sway', YouTube, 6 February. Available online: https://www.youtube.com/watch?v =w28ZREQe3_Q (accessed 7 June 2022).

kazzart (2006), '"Drive" – Bic Runga, Live in London', YouTube, 7 July. Available online: https://www.youtube.com/watch?v=Dm41j3zBatU (accessed 28 January 2021).

King Sweeties (2020), 'Let's Just Stay in Bed', YouTube, 30 April. Available online: https://www.youtube.com/watch?v=75itBVphaH0 (accessed 28 January 2021).

Lorde (2021), *Te Ao Mārama*, EP, Universal Music New Zealand.

New Zealand On Screen (1996), 'Bursting Through'. Available online: https://www.nzonscreen.com/title/bursting-through-1996 (accessed 7 June 2022).

New Zealand On Screen (1997), 'Sway'. Available online: https://www.nzonscreen.com/title/sway-1997 (accessed 18 January 2022).

New Zealand On Screen (2022), *Music Nation*, First Episode. Available online: https://www.nzonscreen.com/title/music-nation-1995-episode (accessed 18 January 2022).

NZ On Air (1996), *Kiwi Talk Disc: A Companion to Kiwi Hit Disc, 18*, Wellington: NZ On Air.

Parnell, Julia and Hinewehi Mohi, producers (2021), 'Waiata/Anthems. Bic Runga: There Is No Time/Kāore He Wā', Season 1, Episode 4. TVNZ. Available online: https://www.tvnz.co.nz/shows/waiata-anthems/episodes/s1-e4 (accessed 22 February 2022).

Radio New Zealand (2017), 'Bic Runga "Bursting Through" Live @ RNZ', 15 September. Available online: https://www.youtube.com/watch?v=htxBYFIiZGg (accessed 5 May 2022).

Radio New Zealand (2020), 'Video Premiere: King Sweeties "Let's Just Stay in Bed"', 30 April. Available online: https://www.rnz.co.nz/national/programmes/nat-music/audio/2018744482/video-premiere-king-sweeties-let-s-just-stay-in-bed (accessed 28 January 2021).

Runga, Bic (1994), 'You', Love Soup Music Video, NZ On Screen. Available online: https://www.nzonscreen.com/title/you-1994 /comments (accessed 22 March 2022).

Runga, Bic (1995), 'Drive', 5-track EP, Epic.

Runga, Bic (1996), 'Bursting Through', Columbia.

Runga, Bic (1997a), *Drive*, Columbia.

Runga, Bic (1997b), 'Roll Into One', Columbia.

Runga, Bic (1997c), 'Suddenly Strange', Columbia.

Runga, Bic (1997d), 'Sway', Columbia.

Runga, Bic (1998), 'Hey', Columbia.

Runga, Bic (1999), *Drive: Limited Edition*, Columbia.

Runga, Bic (2002), *Beautiful Collision*, Columbia.

Runga, Bic (2005), *Birds*, Columbia.

Runga, Bic (2011a), *Belle*, Sony.

Runga, Bic (2011b), 'Bic Runga – Drive', 2 July. Available online: https://www.youtube.com/watch?v=xHGUh30U4tQ (accessed 7 June 2022).

Runga, Bic (2014), 'Bic Runga – Sway (Video Version (US Reshoot))', 23 September. Available online: https://www .youtube.com/watch?v=0S7qa7oJzPg (accessed 7 June 2022).

Runga, Bic (2016), *Close Your Eyes*, Sony.

Runga, Bic (2017a), 'Bic Runga – Bursting Through', 6 January. Available online: https://www.youtube.com/watch?v =MVYFgJo5cgM (accessed 7 June 2022).

Runga, Bic (2017b), 'Bic Runga – Suddenly Strange', 6 January. Available online: https://www.youtube.com/watch?v =3NfpddJ1pn8 (accessed 7 June 2022).

Runga, Bic (2017c), *Drive: 20th Anniversary Edition*, Sony Music.

Runga, Bic, Tim Finn and Dave Dobbyn (2000), *Together in Concert: Live*, CRS/Epic.

Simon, Paul (1986), *Graceland*, Warner Bros.

Various Artists (1995a), *Kiwi Hit Disc 12*, NZ On Air.

Various Artists (1995b), *Kiwi Talk Disc: A Companion to Kiwi Hit Disc 12*, NZ On Air.

Various Artists (1998), *Lilith Fair '98: A Starbucks Blend CD*, EMI-Capitol.

Various Artists (1999), *Lilith Fair (A Celebration of Women in Music)*, Vol. 2, Arista.

Various Artists (2002), *Nature's Best: New Zealand's Top 30 Songs of All-Time*, Sony.

Various Artists (2004), *Even Better than the Real Thing*, Vol. 2, RMG.

*Waiata/Anthems* (2019), Universal Music New Zealand.

Wright, Geoffrey, dir. (1992), *Romper Stomper*, Film Victoria.

# Acknowledgements

I would like to thank several individuals and organizations who have helped make this book possible. In particular, I thank Bic Runga for generously answering my interview questions and offering valuable insight into her music and professional career. Other personnel involved in Runga's early work have offered comment on many facets of the music business at the time, and I am especially grateful to Trevor Reekie and Andrew Thorne for their informative insight.

Several illustrations are included in the book as a way of offering visual imagery from the mid-1990s around the release of *Drive*. Two magazine images were reproduced from hard copies held in the Hocken Library and with the help of Richard Munro. The image from *Rip It Up* was provided with permission by Simon Grigg, and the photographer, Cindy Wilson, is gratefully acknowledged. The image from *New Zealand Musician* is reproduced with permission from Richard Thorne and photographer Tony Nyberg. A further image is reproduced with permission from Stuff Limited and photographer Melanie Burford. I thank Jude Tewnion, the National Library of New Zealand and Natalie Marshall for making this possible. While many of the recordings under study are in my personal collection, others (especially singles and promotional releases) were listened to with the help of Michael Brown, Mark Hector, Ian Brailsford, University of Otago, Alexander Turnbull Library,

National Library of New Zealand, and Auckland University Libraries and Learning Services.

I would like to thank editors Jon Stratton and Jon Dale and everyone at Bloomsbury who has contributed to the production of the book in many ways. I am especially grateful to the University of Otago for providing funding to help with the completion of the book, to Peter Adams for offering comments on some of *Drive*'s musical detail, and to Lisa Marr for assistance and compiling the index. Lastly, thank you also to the anonymous readers who provided valuable feedback, and to Ian Chapman and Lisa for their excellent suggestions on the manuscript. Any errors in the book, however, are entirely my own.

**Acknowledgements**

# Appendix 1
## *Drive*: Track listing and personnel

| Track | Title | Duration |
|-------|-------|----------|
| 1 | 'Drive' | 2'48" |
| | Bic Runga: vocals, guitar | |
| 2 | 'Sway' | 4'24" |
| | Bic Runga: vocals, xylophone, backing vocals | |
| | Gary Verberne: guitars | |
| | Aaron McDonald: bass | |
| | Kate Walshe: violin | |
| | Sally-Anne Brown: cello | |
| | Andrew Thorne: guitars | |
| | Wayne Bell: drums | |
| | Duncan Haynes: string arrangement | |
| | Nick Seymour: additional arrangement | |
| | Niall Macken: additional arrangement | |
| 3 | 'Hey' | 3'16" |
| | Bic Runga: vocals, xylophone, backing vocals | |
| | Andrew Thorne: guitars | |

*(Continued)*

| Track | Title | Duration |
|-------|-------|----------|
| | Aaron McDonald: bass | |
| | Wayne Bell: drums | |
| 4 | 'Bursting Through' | 3'42" |
| | Bic Runga: vocals, guitar | |
| | Andrew Thorne: guitar | |
| | Kate Walshe: violin | |
| | Sarah Yates: strings | |
| | Wayne Bell: drums, percussion | |
| | Duncan Haynes: string arrangement | |
| | Karl Steven: additional arrangement | |
| 5 | 'Swim' | 4'44" |
| | Bic Runga: vocals | |
| | Andrew Thorne: guitars | |
| | Aaron McDonald: bass | |
| | Wayne Bell: drums | |
| | Boh Runga: backing vocals | |
| | Malcolm Smith: keyboards | |
| 6 | 'Roll Into One' | 3'19" |
| | Bic Runga: vocals, guitar | |
| | Andrew Thorne: guitars, backing vocals | |
| | Aaron McDonald: bass | |
| | Wayne Bell: drums | |
| | Matt Wallace: guitar, backing vocals | |
| | Peter Asher: backing vocals | |
| | Boh Runga: backing vocals | |

| Track | Title | Duration |
|-------|-------|----------|
| 7 | 'Suddenly Strange' | 4'19" |
| | Bic Runga: vocals, guitar, mellotron, backing vocals | |
| | Josh Freese: drums | |
| | Davey Fargher: bass | |
| | Matt Wallace: percussion | |
| | Kate Walshe: violin | |
| | Sally-Anne Brown: cello | |
| | Duncan Haynes: string arrangement | |
| | Nick Seymour: additional arrangement | |
| | Niall Macken: additional arrangement | |
| 8 | 'Sorry' | 3'24" |
| | Bic Runga: vocals, drums | |
| | Andrew Thorne: guitars | |
| | Aaron McDonald: bass | |
| | Jay Foulkes: percussion | |
| 9 | 'Heal' | 3'33" |
| | Bic Runga: vocals, guitar | |
| | Andrew Thorne: guitar | |
| | Aaron McDonald: bass | |
| | Wayne Bell: drums | |
| | Paul Casserly: samples | |
| | Malcolm Smith: keyboards, additional samples | |

*(Continued)*

| Track | Title | Duration |
|-------|-------|----------|
| 10 | 'Delight' | 4'01" |
| | Bic Runga: vocals | |
| | Andrew Thorne: guitar | |
| | Aaron McDonald: bass | |
| | Wayne Bell: drums | |
| | Paul Casserly: samples | |
| | Duncan Haynes: Rhodes | |
| 11 | 'Without You' | 4'01" |
| | Bic Runga: vocals, xylophone, backing vocals | |
| | Gary Verberne: guitars | |
| | Andrew Thorne: guitars, backing vocals | |
| | Aaron McDonald: bass | |
| | Wayne Bell: drums | |
| | Nick Seymour: additional arrangement | |
| | Niall Macken: additional arrangement | |

Mastered by Matt Wallace.

Produced by Bic Runga.

Engineered by Simon Sheridan (assisted by Matt Tait) except 'Drive', engineered by Chris van de Geer, and 'Suddenly Strange', engineered by Simon Sheridan (assisted by Matt Tait) and Matt Wallace (assisted by Tom Banghart).

Mixed by Matt Wallace (assisted by Tom Banghart) except 'Drive', mixed by Bic Runga.

All songs written and arranged by Bic Runga.

Bic Runga managed by Campbell Smith.

Art Direction: Wayne Conway.
Design: The Family.
Photography: Cindy Wilson.

Source: Runga (1997a).

NB. The booklet with the liner notes gives the order of the last three tracks as: 'Without You', 'Delight' and 'Heal'.

# Appendix 2
## Bic Runga: Discography (New Zealand album releases)

| Studio albums | Date | Label |
|---|---|---|
| *Drive* | 1997 | Columbia |
| *Beautiful Collision* | 2002 | Columbia |
| *Birds* | 2005 | Columbia |
| *Belle* | 2011 | Sony |
| *Close Your Eyes* | 2016 | Sony |
| *Drive: 20th Anniversary Edition* | 2017 | Sony |
| **Compilation albums** | | |
| *Try to Remember Everything* | 2008 | Columbia |
| *Anthology* | 2012 | Sony |
| *The Very Best of Bic Runga* | 2017 | Sony |
| **Live album** | | |
| *Together in Concert: Live (Tim Finn, Bic Runga, Dave Dobbyn)* | 2000 | Epic |

# Index